CAROLINA BLUEGRASS

A HIGH LONESOME HISTORY

GAIL WILSON-GIARRATANO, PhD

Foreword by Larry Klein and Pat Ahrens

THE
History
PRESS

Published by The History Press
Charleston, SC
www.historypress.net

Front cover, top right: Wayne Benson. *Photograph by Blake Williams; courtesy of Wayne Benson.*
Back cover, top: Bill Wells and the Blue Ridge Mountain Grass. *Courtesy of Louise Wells*; *bottom left*: Ashley Carder relatives, circa 1870s. *Courtesy of Ashley Carder.*

First published 2015

Manufactured in the United States

ISBN 978.1.46711.824.8

Library of Congress Control Number: 2015949248

Notice: The information in this book is true and complete to the best of our knowledge. It is offered without guarantee on the part of the author or The History Press. The author and The History Press disclaim all liability in connection with the use of this book.

Contents

Foreword

Bluegrass is a musical genre that was born from music first sung around the house, farm and church and passed along through the oral tradition from generation to generation. Although it became a successful commercial musical form, to this day it remains strongly rooted in traditional musical skills that are learned by word of mouth, observation and listening. As such, it is a living, breathing art form given life by its many practitioners and by the very act of passing the music along. In these pages, you will meet Carolina musicians who all have a story to tell; some are professionals, some are serious tradition bearers and some are simply enjoying the social nature of the music.

Music is so woven into the fabric of our lives that it is sometimes taken for granted. The folks that you'll meet here are among the ones who will never let the art of making music die. Tradition is a cornerstone of stability in our lives. For as long as man sings, his voice will echo throughout the universe and the world will be a better place.

Many of the people you'll see in these photographs have devoted a large part of their lives to making music. Some have actively taught, and some have unknowingly inspired others along the way. It is like a huge "living" concentric circle with a feeling of kinship at its core.

For more than a quarter of a century, Bill's Music Shop & Pickin' Parlor, established from the vision of the late Bill Wells, has been a South Carolina epicenter for bluegrass. Young and old, professional and amateur, performer and listener, singer and dancer, all have come together in this place dedicated to the preservation of the whole of bluegrass. Bill Wells received the Order of the Palmetto, South Carolina's highest civilian honor, in recognition of the importance of his contributions. You will hear from many of those associated with Bill's Music Shop in this book.

In North Carolina, the Tar Heels have given the music many of the most important festivals in existence, from the state's annual Old Time Fiddlers Convention to folk-gatherings dating back to the 1920s. Modern festivals, such as Merlefest in Wilkesboro, bring together state, national and international performers for huge appreciative audiences. These festivals have become a "melting pot" for bluegrass music. North Carolina is home to many professional groups that perform nationally. The wealth of its old-time folk music and instrument craft traditions are widely renowned and studied by folklorists and artisans from around the world.

The people appearing in these pages are Carolinians who bring acoustic instruments to life and make it possible for you to hear the ancient tones of the fiddle, metronomic chop of the mandolin, the powerful drive of the banjo, the mellow strum of the guitar, the bluesy sound of the Dobro® and the steady rhythm of the bass…played all together, they make bluegrass.

Bill Monroe is widely acknowledged as the father of bluegrass music. His musical career spanned more than a half century. Monroe's career encompassed an era of tremendous change in American popular entertainment, all the way from the primitive "kerosene circuit" to early radio and the burgeoning recording industry to television and film, as well as the Internet and YouTube. Much of Monroe's early professional career took place in and many of the gifted musicians he hired for his band were strongly based in North and South Carolina. The Carolinas helped as much as anywhere to shape the sound of bluegrass music.

Monroe's music was music that came straight from the "true life stories" of farmers, coal miners, lumberjacks, railroad gangs, mill workers, storekeepers and steady wage earners. These were the hands that worked to give us bluegrass's "High Lonesome Sound." Monroe sang and played straight from the heart of America while delivering a sophisticated sound to an incredible diversity of people, truly unique in the scope of its breadth and appeal.

So we certainly hope that you will enjoy these personal stories and insights into Bluegrass music in the Carolinas as much as we do. Although this music has become international, its very heart and soul remain centered in North and South Carolina.

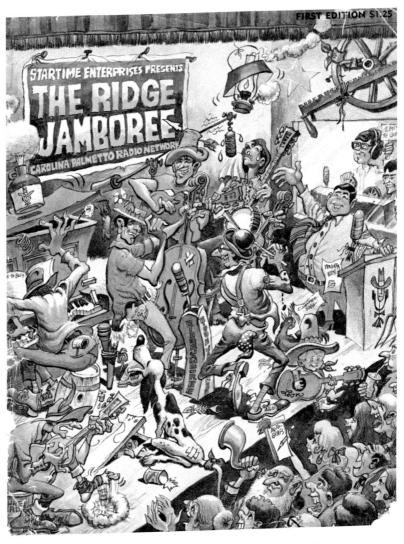

Program cover of the *Ridge Jamboree* circa 1969. *Courtesy of Ashley Carder.*

An inadequate but sincere thank you goes to Gail Wilson-Giarratano for her interest in the music, her many hours of interviews and phone calls and for caring enough to get it all written down.

PAT J. AHRENS

Author and bluegrass historian, emcee for the weekly "Open Stage" at Bill's Music Shop & Pickin' Parlor and 1996 recipient of the Jean Laney

FOREWORD

Harris Folk Heritage Award from the South Carolina Arts Commission and Legislature

DR. LARRY KLEIN

Host of South Carolina Public Radio's *The Bluegrass Sound* and *Guitars, Cadillacs and Hillbilly Music*; Dobro® player with the Blue Ridge Mountain Grass, Amick Junction, Palmetto Blue and the Carolina Rebels; and 1996 recipient of the Jean Laney Harris Folk Heritage Award from the South Carolina Arts Commission and Legislature

Acknowledgements

Bluegrass music is powerful medicine.
—Wayne Benson

I'd like to thank everyone who provided information, support, feedback, guidance and inspiration for this project. When I began writing this book, I had one or perhaps two bluegrass friends. Today, I have come to know and respect several dozen bluegrass musicians and champions, and they have welcomed me into their circle. This book is a chronicle of my efforts to honor the Carolina bluegrass circle and make it a bit wider in the process.

Special thanks go to Martha Adcock, Pat Ahrens, Cindy and Terry Baucom, Roger Bellow, Wayne and Kristin Scott Benson, Alan Bibey, Curtis Blackwell, Chris Bouthwell, Sarah Bryan, Ashley Carder, Danny Creamer, Shellie Davis, Ed Dover, Gary Erwin, Jim Graddick, Hastings Hensel, Roger Howell, Richard Hurley, Larry Klein, Shirley Landsdown, Ted Lehmann, Annette and Harold Lucas, Randy and Bailee Lucas, Tony McKie, Katie Miller, Carolina Rose, Louise and Willie Wells, "Uncle" Ted White and the entire Bill's Pickin' Parlor family. I extend my deep appreciation to Chad Rhoad, senior acquisitions editor and The History Press; Julia Turner, production editor; and The History Press team for their creativity, hard work and dedication. Special gratitude goes to Gloria Glickman for her clerical and administrative support, and Careese Robinson for his digital photography. I am grateful to my family: Marvin and Harriet Wilson; Kitty and John Evans; and Vanessa, Rob and

ACKNOWLEDGEMENTS

Pepper Wilson-Maurice. Finally, to my loving husband, Anthony Charles (Giarratano), thank you for your knowledge, experience and patience. Special love goes to Adelina Bambina, R.A.G. and Sergio forever.

Introduction

On April 9, 2015, I had just left my office in downtown Columbia, South Carolina, to make a stop at Pat Ahrens's house for a helpin' of some good ol' bluegrass schoolin'. Pat, a noted bluegrass historian and longtime champion of the genre, had become both a mentor and friend. Pat generously offered her personal archives in an effort to help me understand what she came to understand many years ago. According to Pat, "Bluegrass is the kind of music that you either love or hate. If you don't love it, you can be taught to appreciate it. But it will never become part of your soul."

Pat maintains a meticulous treasure-trove of bluegrass books, articles, posters and memorabilia. Literally every bookshelf, drawer and file cabinet in her beautifully decorated home is utilized to hold the bluegrass collection, which brings her great joy and pride. I'll never forget the first time she invited me to her home. As she greeted me at the door, white hair perfectly coiffed, blue eyes sparkling, she cheerfully told me she had pulled out "a few things" for me to look at and laid them out on the guest room bed. When we reached the room, my jaw dropped. If there was a bed under all the books and files, I'd be doggone if I could find it! Anyone seeking information about the bluegrass of North and South Carolina will at some point need to call on Pat Ahrens.

This particular evening, we were seated at Pat's kitchen table. She had prepared folders containing notes and assignments for me, the list of people I needed to call and articles to read. I sat sipping a ginger ale while Pat

Pat Ahrens's bluegrass collection. *Photograph by Careese Robinson.*

read out loud from her favorite book about Bill Monroe, the father of bluegrass music. Suddenly, she snapped the book closed, pulled out a CD and continued the conversation. "Now, I need you to listen to some music." She clicked on the small CD player that sat on the kitchen table.

The music was the haunting melody of the instrumental "Oconee." The beautiful song included not one but three masterful mandolins and was written by her longtime friend Tut Taylor.

Tut Taylor named the song in honor of the Oconee River in Georgia, where he had grown up. As a young man he taught himself to play a Dobro® with a flat pick because he simply didn't know that's not how it was done. The result was a unique sound that became his trademark and earned him the name "the flat pickin' Dobro® man."

Mr. Taylor played with dozens of pickers during his long career, including Norman Blake, John Hartford, Sam Bush, Curtis Burch, Butch Robins, Tom McKinney, Rual Yarbrough, Randy Wood, Jim Johnson, Leon Russel, Vassar Clements, Porter Wagoner, Ron and Don Norman, Hughie Wylie, Clarence and Roland White, Bill Monroe, Bennie Martin, Don Reno and J.N. and Onie Baxter. Bands included the Bluegrass Five, the Season Travelers, the Smoky Mountain Boys and the iconic "newgrass" Aereo-Plain band. They were the first bluegrass band to ever play with a symphony orchestra. Tut was quoted as saying, "Pickin' has been a great part of my life, not financially rewarding, but a lot of fun."

Pat explained that she first met Tut Taylor around 1967 while attending the Union Grove, North Carolina Old Time Fiddlers Convention. The friendship continued to grow as Pat and Tut would find themselves at festivals and events throughout the region. Pat said, "This was back during the time when musicians like Tut were just beginning to make their mark." During the 1970s, Pat would make the trip to Nashville to the Old Time Pickin' Parlor, a downtown hot spot that Tut helped to start. Pat, like many lovers of traditional and bluegrass music, found that this was the place to be if you wanted to hear musicians like Tut Taylor, John Harford, Charlie Collins, Neal Young and Norman Blake. The Parlor's casual setting was the perfect backdrop for old-time, country, blues and bluegrass music. Amateurs and professionals, fans and friends would gather to swap musical licks and laughter. Pat felt right at home and said, "The Old Time Pickin' Parlor was going like wildfire in its day."

Long after the Pickin' Parlor quieted down, Pat remained good friends with Tut, who was by then living in Knoxville. Several times a year, Tut and his friends, loosely termed the "Georgia Boys," would host parties for sixty to seventy musicians and friends. They would come together, socialize and play music with and for each other. Tut, also a talented visual artist and sign painter by trade, often created hand-painted invitations for such events. Pat would sometimes receive a personal invitation, which she saved in her rapidly growing keepsake collection. She enjoyed attending the parties to hear music, eat barbecue and pick. She said:

> *Tut could just play anything and do it in so many ways. He was an instrument builder and artist; he was just one of those people who was the whole ball of wax. Tut had a true interest in vintage instruments at a time when only people in major cities like New York or Boston were repairing stringed instruments. He was one of the people that developed the art and business of fine instrument repair in this area. The way he approached everything was special; it was almost spiritual.*

By 2001, Pat was convinced that she needed to write a book in honor of Tut and his accomplishments. She would travel to Knoxville for interviews, have lengthy phone conversations and make sure that she taped and documented everything. Her book, *Tut Taylor, the Flat Pickin' Dobro® Man* (2003), shares highlights about the musicianship and artistry of Tut Taylor.

Tut Taylor, the flat pickin' Dobro® man. *Courtesy of Pat Ahrens.*

According to Pat, "I've been privy to some beautiful moments in the history of this music. Tut and all these exceptional artists are able to communicate in ways that [the] average person could never do."

As we sat at the kitchen table and continued to listen to Tut's music, she gestured to the refrigerator, which was covered with photographs of various

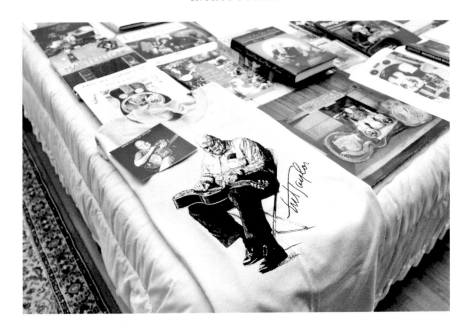

Above: Tut Taylor souvenir T-shirt. *Courtesy of Pat Ahrens.*

Right: Tut Taylor crafted Grammy Dobro Bluegrass Collage. *Courtesy of Pat Ahrens.*

Personal party invitation drawn by Tut Taylor. *Courtesy of Pat Ahrens.*

musicians and newspaper clippings. "That's Tut," she said pointing to the eight-by-ten color photograph. The music filled the kitchen as Pat sat, her eyes closed, and then whispered softly, "Tut's one of the most talented men I have ever met." It was clear she not only respected the musicianship but also valued the friendship. However, what Pat and I didn't know was that earlier that very morning Tut Taylor passed away at the Wilkes Regional Medical Center in North Carolina. He was ninety-one.

PART I

I HEARD A BANJAR PLAYIN'

I
(Re)Birth of the Banjo

The banjo and fiddle have been as constant companions of the pioneers of the
mountains of North Carolina as the Bible and the Hymn Book.
—John Peterson Arthur (1851–1916)

The five-string banjo, long associated with Old Time American music used by Earl Scruggs and Bela Fleck, represents the most familiar and popular type of banjo used in bluegrass music. According to banjo historian George Gibson, the earliest reference to the banjo in the Carolinas he found was from the 1780s in a quote that described how Carolinians were dancing to the banjo and fiddle before the Civil War. The banjo originated over one hundred years ago on the continent of Africa. The original African stringed instrument was simple and rough, traditionally made of animal skin tacked on to one half of a hollowed gourd. The instrument's strings were three or four strands of waxed horsehair or gut stretched over a stick. Scholars have found that names for these early African instruments include "banjar," "banjil," "banza," "bangoe," "bangie" and "banshaw." Some historians mention the diaries of Richard Jobson as the first record of the instrument. While exploring the Gambra River in Africa in 1620, he recorded an instrument that was "made of a great gourd and a neck, thereunto was fastened strings." One of the best-known references to the banjo is that of Thomas Jefferson in 1781: "The instrument proper to them (i.e. the slaves) is the Banjar, which they brought hither from Africa."

According to Robert Lloyd, the early black banjo players combined African tones and rhythm to ballads and hymns brought from England, Ireland and Scotland.

Drawing on the Scotch-Irish dance tunes, English ballads and African American traditional five-string banjo melodies, white musicians, such as Joel "Joe" Walker Sweeney, learned to play the banjo. Sweeny was born in Buckingham County, Virginia, in 1810 and is known as the leader of the Virginia Minstrel. Sweeney was born in a log cabin located near the site where the Civil War ended.

Although Sweeney has been credited widely with introducing the fifth string on the banjo, a painting entitled *The Old Plantation*, painted between 1777 and 1800, shows a laborer playing a gourd-banjo with five strings. According to a 1969 article in *The Iron Worker*, Joel Walker Sweeney learned to play a four-string gourd banjo at age thirteen from the field hands working on the family farm. Sweeny might not have actually invented the five-string banjo. However, his comedic impressions of plantation life through the use of blackface and vaudeville had an audience. Popular minstrel shows introduced the banjo to people around the United States and Europe. Joel traveled throughout central Virginia in the early 1830s, playing his five-string banjo, singing, reciting and imitating animals with the Virginia Minstrels. The group consisted of two banjo players—Dan Emmett and Billy Whitlock, a pupil of Sweeney—as well as a fiddler, a bones player and a drum or tambourine player.

George Gibson argues that Dan Emmett, who claimed authorship of songs such as "Dixie," might have actually borrowed the songs from the traditional music of black families he befriended. The blending of white and black music took place long before the minstrel performers of the 1840s. Gibson said, "The folk banjo was mostly a rural and southern instrument."

Josiah Combs was born in Knott County, Kentucky, and received his doctorate at the University of Paris in 1952. His dissertation, "Folk-Songs of the Southern United States," includes a list of African American banjo songs that were introduced to Kentucky musicians by black banjo players before the Civil War. Minstrel performers were successful in the United States and traveled through Europe and the British Isles. They performed in circuses and comedy shows, venues where the focus was on entertainment, not musicianship. Some of the wealthy and well-to-do members of society, especially in the North, snubbed the banjo. Articles in the papers of the day like that in the *Boston Daily Evening Voice* of 1866 referred to the banjo of the 1840s and 1850s as an instrument in "the depth of popular degradation, an instrument fit only for the jig-dancing lower classes of the community."

During the 1930s, the Federal Writers' Project located former slaves and recorded their oral histories. Belinda Hurmence transcribed interviews with 284 former South Carolina slaves for the book *Before Freedom, When I Just Can Remember*. Many of these interviews provide insight to the complex relationship between slave owners, slaves and music. One example is included in an excerpt from this 1936 interview with Brawley Gilmore from Union, South Carolina: "Dr. McCollum, Doc, he rid a white pony called Fannie. Doc, he liked to fiddle. Old Fannie, she would get up on her hind legs when Doc would play his fiddle."

According to Allen Farmelo, a New York scholar, many early bluegrass festivals and clubs tended to be segregated and the music associated with the racial attitudes of the old South.

Groups such as the Carolina Chocolate Drops and artists like Bela Fleck have worked to bring greater awareness to the interconnectedness of African American culture and old-time music in the South. Bela Fleck's documentary, *Throw Down Your Heart*, demonstrated that songs such as "Rocky Top" and "Foggy Mountain Breakdown" are similar to songs still played in Africa. Fleck said, "I thought it was important for people to realize where the banjo comes from." Kristin Scott Benson of the "Grascals" stated:

> *I think the music community, in general, has always been a common place where you can see racial and socioeconomic walls crumble. For bluegrass, I think the bottom line is that the people who like it and are drawn to it, just happen to be predominantly white. That's interesting because the banjo is an African instrument and it's highly documented and pretty much indisputable that Bill Monroe was influenced by African American roots music. We share so much, I'm surprised we haven't seen more integration in bluegrass, or in churches, for that matter.*

Appalachian folk music has had a major influence on the development of both the country and bluegrass styles. One of the earliest collectors of Appalachian ballads was John Jacob Niles, a Kentucky native, who began noting ballads as early as 1907. Niles recorded examples of the ballads in Boone, Saluda and Greenville, South Carolina.

In 1916, Cecil Sharp, a British folklorist, came to America to study the traditional songs and dances after World War I. Sharp identified and recorded 1,600 versions of five hundred songs from 281 singers. The majority of the songs he studied came directly from the families living in the area of Shelton Laurel, North Carolina. After his first visit to America, Sharp published his book, *English Folk Songs from the Southern Appalachians*. Cecil Sharp became an authority on hillbilly (as it was known) music and hillbilly life.

Some say that the word hillbilly directly referred to those settlers in the hill country of Appalachia. The subject of the early songs was William, Prince of Orange, at the Battle of the Boyne, Ireland, in 1690. Supporters of King William were known as "Billy Boys." Once these immigrants settled in America, a combination of the geographical region and the Irish ancestry resulted in a new term, "hill-billies." Also, many of the Tennessee, North Carolina and Virginia settlers chose to name their sons in honor of King William by naming them "Bill."

Sharp, however, was not the only folklorist interested in what was taking place in "hills and hollers" of North Carolina. Bascom Lamar Lunsford was a North Carolina native son who made a tremendous contribution of his own.

Lunsford was born in 1882, in Madison County just north of Asheville, North Carolina. He took up the fiddle and banjo as a child and loved the mountain ballads and hymns his mother would sing around the house. It wasn't long before he became a familiar musician around town, playing at local social events. Lunsford played a unique style of banjo similar to the traditional claw-hammer style of mountain picking. He also played a "mandoline," an instrument with a mandolin body and a five-string banjo neck. Lunsford and other noted banjo players in North Carolina, such as Frank Noah Proffitt, inspired musicians to play the instrument

Lunsford was interested in preserving the music he loved so much. He was a songwriter, recorded the music of others in the area and became known as a "song collector."

His talents and interests extended beyond music to include business and professional ventures. He worked as a fruit tree salesman, traveled with a Cherokee beekeeper and even served as an agent assigned to chasing draft evaders.

In 1909, after graduating from Rutherford College he became a teacher. Later, he went back to school to study law, passed the bar in 1913 and worked for several years with the North Carolina legislature. You could say that Bascom Lamar Lunsford was a man with "a whole lot of gumption." According to Asheville native, singer-songwriter Richard Hurley:

Bascom Lamar Lunsford was the "Minstrel of the Appalachians" who is responsible for perpetuating the old-time music of the Southern Appalachians. He was a lawyer, a gentleman farmer and quite a cultural icon. Mars Hill University possesses many of his archives and annually produces the Lunsford Festival, which I traditionally emcee and participate in. I feature him in a cut, from my perspective, on my CD, which basically tells the story of the Mountain Dance and Folk Festival, which he started in 1928. It's the longest-running folk festival in the nation and the event from which the Shindig was spawned.

I met him a time or two but did not play the festival until 1982 or so, about nine years after his death. My brother, Jim Ab, worked for a local newspaper and did a nice article about him in the early '60s. Mr. Lunsford recorded hundreds of songs from memory for the Library of Congress.

Bascom Lamar Lunsford (left), founder of Asheville, North Carolina Folk Heritage Festival
Courtesy of Pat Ahrens.

CAROLINA BLUEGRASS

Bascom Lamar Lunsford is remembered for his constant fight against the derogatory stereotype associated with backcountry musicians and "hillbilly music." He recorded thousands of songs for the Smithsonian, and in the summer of 1928, he created the Asheville Mountain Dance and Folk Festival. The event, which still continues today, is considered to be the first bluegrass festival.

The Ballad of Bascom Lamar Lunsford
© 2004 Richard Hurley

In eighteen hundred and eighty-two
Bascom was born where the mountain air blows cool.
A gentleman farmer and a lawyer man
This Minstrel of The Mountains loved God's green land.
A man with a vision—and a love for the past,
He made sure the dances and the ballads would last.
Preserving our culture and our music so pure—
The hollers and the coves were his constant lure.
He gathered up folks—some young and some old—
There were dancers and singers and pickers I'm told.
In the year twenty-eight here in Asheville town
A festival was born—'long about sundown.
Bascom was a mentor to all who were eager
Including a legend—the folk singer, Pete Seeger.
People would come from across our great land
To hear the sweet music of a real mountain band.
In his bright white suit, he would kick up his feet
Near the edge of the stage never missing a beat.
Calling up the children, he'd let each one play—
Now all grown up; some are legends today.
The fiddle and the ballad and the banjo, too,
There was Obrey and Byard to name just a few.
Samantha would pick and Tommy would bow
While Glenn led the dancers through a smooth dosey-doe.
The cloggers kept rhythm to the banjo ring—
Luke played the fiddle and Betty would sing
Red played the mouth harp stuck back in his jaw—
And it beat anything that a body ever saw!
He learned many songs and he penned him a few—

The most famous one was "Old Mountain Dew."
Now Stoney Creek plays as the house band nowadays,
And Bascom would smile were he with us I'd say.
Many are gone now who once took the stage—
Grover and Carroll—you could fill up a page.
Grandson, Ed Herron, remembers his granddad,
His charm, his wit, and the good times they had.
His life had a purpose and a mission, you see;
And Bascom passed on back in seventy-three.
But his legacy lives on and his spirit's all around
The first weekend in August—'long about sundown!

By 1910, industrialists had succeeded in capturing a large segment of the New England textile mill industry. In 1880, there were 161 mills in the South. However, by 1900, there were over 400 mills in four southern states: North Carolina, South Carolina, Georgia and Alabama. By 1923, 351 mills were located in North Carolina alone; more than eighty-one thousand employees were women and children.

Mill owners and politicians were eager to promote the mills, claiming the benefits of steady pay and housing. However, poor southern families often found themselves trapped into working in the mills for their entire lives. Forced to help provide for their families, children received minimal education while sometimes suffering terrible injuries, such as severed fingers or limbs or developing Brown Lung disease. The workdays were long, starting at 6:00 a.m. and continuing until 6:00 p.m., six days a week.

Documenting conditions at the North Carolina textile mills in the 1930s, historians collected many stories from millworkers. Alice P. Evitt described the dangers she and others faced when operating these machines:

> *I'd get my apron tore off of me in the speeder room—when I was learnin'*
> *to run speeders, I'd get my apron tore off of me two or three times a week.*
> *They'd wind me up and I was just lucky I managed to stop 'em and didn't*
> *get my arms in them. Them fliers would break your bones…I know one*
> *lady, I didn't see her get it done, but she said she wore wigs and she'd get her*
> *hair caught and it pulled her whole scalp out, every bit of her hair.*

Yet these hardworking, determined men and women found ways to support one another through difficult and unbearable times by creating a village within the mill. If anyone were sick, women would organize a "pounding."

This collective effort was described as neighbors taking turns contributing a pound of sugar, butter or food to the home of the family in need.

Historians noted that through this "unique workers' culture," mill hands created their own sense of family out of the mill community. Rural families in the South replicated the kinship patterns in the mill villages that had long sustained them, sometimes with real kin, other times with neighbors and friends.

Before radio, men would gather on their precious day off and play banjo, fiddle and guitar for church services, weddings and social entertainment. The most talented musicians gained tremendous respect and status within their mill village and the surrounding area through music.

DORSEY DIXON (1897–1968)

Dorsey Murdock Dixon, born in Darlington, South Carolina, was one of seven children. His father operated a steam engine at the Darlington Cotton Manufacturing Company. Dorsey left school after the fourth grade to work in the mill. He loved music and was given violin lessons and taught himself to play the guitar by the time he was fourteen. Between 1919 and 1927, he moved to Lancaster, South Carolina, and Richmond County, North Carolina, searching for work. He secured employment at the Aleo Mill in East Rockingham, North Carolina. Dorsey was deeply impacted by a terrible fire in a school in Cleveland, South Carolina, and began writing poetry about this and other events. The 1929 textile mill strike in Gastonia, along with unsatisfactory living and working conditions, became the subject of his writing as well as his music.

Dorsey and his brother Howard were noticed by Fisher Hendley, a musician and talent scout for radio station WBT in Charlotte. In 1934, Hendley invited the brothers to become part of J.W. Fincher's *Crazy Water Crystals Saturday Night Jamboree*. Although success of songs such as "Weaver's Life," "Intoxicated Rat," "I Didn't Hear Anybody Pray" and "Wreck on the Highway" were popular, they were clouded under copyright confusion. Dorsey received little financial benefits from his songs, so broke and frustrated, the Dixon brothers went back to work in the mills until 1951.

Folklorists Archie Gree, Ed Kahn and Gene Earle met Dixon in 1962 and helped record a new album of his music. As part of the folk revival movement, Dixon was invited to the 1963 Newport Folk Festival. The poetic lyrics will always be a reminder of the hardships at the Carolina mills.

I HEARD A BANJAR PLAYIN'

Weave Room Blues by Dorsey Dixon (1932)

Working in a weave-room, fighting for my life
Trying to make a living for my kiddies and my wife;
Some are needing clothing, some are needing shoes,
But I'm getting nothing but the weave-room blues.
I've got the blues, I've got the blues,
I've got them awful weave-room blues;
I got the blues, the weave-room blues.
With your looms a-slamming, shuttles bouncing in the floor,
When you flag your fixer, you can see that he is sore;
Trying to make a living, but I'm thinking I will lose,
For I'm sent a-dying with them weave-room blues.
I've got the blues, I've got the blues,
I've got them awful weave-room blues;
I got the blues, the weave-room blues.
Harness eyes are breaking with the doubles coming through,

Vintage fiddler. *Courtesy of Bill's Music Shop & Pickin' Parlor & Willie Wells.*

Mountain family members and friends. *Courtesy of Louise Wells.*

Devil's in your alley and he's coming after you,
Our hearts are aching, well, let's take a little booze;
For we're simply dying with them weave-room blues.
I've got the blues, got the blues,
I've got them awful weave-room blues;
I got the blues, the weave-room blues.
Slam-outs, break-outs, knot-ups by the score,
Cloth all rolled back and piled up in the floor;
The harness eyes are breaking, strings are hanging to your shoes,
We're simply dying with them weave-room blues.
I've got the blues, got the blues,
I've got them awful weave-room blues;
I got the blues, the weave-room blues.

2

You Can Only Get There from Here

The contributions of Carolina musicians born between the years 1908 and 1924 to the developments in old-time and bluegrass music have been widely documented. Carolinians are fortunate to have excellent resource books, articles, journals and websites that detail the lives and music of these legends. In this chapter, I will offer a broad overview of the contributions of a few of these musicians and encourage you to continue to learn more about their significant accomplishments by reading the works of dedicated authors, folklorist and historians who continue to preserve their legacies and promote bluegrass music.

Dewitt "Snuffy" Jenkins (1908–1990)

Dewitt "Snuffy" Jenkins was born on October 27, 1908, in Harris, North Carolina, not far from the city of Shelby. He grew up hearing the distinctive three-finger banjo style played by amateur musicians in that part of the Piedmont. According to an October 1977 interview for *Bluegrass Unlimited*, conducted by Tony Trischka, Dewitt "Snuffy" Jenkins said:

> *There was seven of us in the family and, of course, just about all of them played a little bit, not much professionally, but me and my brother Verl, we played more together than anybody, and he was a fiddler and I was playing the banjo. We had a band of our own. I was actually playing guitar a little*

Dewitt "Snuffy" Jenkins. This is the cover image of Pat Ahrens's book *Legacy of Two Legends. Photographer Jock Lauterer; courtesy of Bill's Music Shop & Pickin' Parlor & Willie Wells.*

bit before I got to playing the banjo. And we were playing for dances and fiddlers' conventions around in the twenties.

Jenkins switched to guitar and later to a homemade banjo he and his brother Verl built. He did not purchase his first real banjo until 1927 and was influenced by the music of Smith Hammett and Rex Brooks. In 1934, Jenkins became the first to use the new style on radio, debuting on WBT's Crazy Water Barn Dance. Promotional material noted that they were "playing the old-time mountain tunes like very few can, and in that 'peppy' style that is peculiarly their own." After a brief stint as bandleader, Jenkins joined J.E. Mainer's Mountaineers, one of the period's most popular string bands, and broadcast with them over WSPA Spartanburg and WIS Columbia.

In August 1937, Jenkins put his three-finger banjo style on record. In a drapery-shrouded room on the tenth floor of the Hotel Charlotte, he and the Mountaineers recorded with J.E. on fiddle, George Morris on guitar and Leonard Stokes on mandolin. The sound "came frightfully close to bluegrass," wrote folklorists Ivan Tribe and John Morris, despite the fact that Bill Monroe was still two years from forming his first bluegrass group. Snuffy Jenkins also influenced Earl Scruggs and Don Reno. According to the book *The Charlotte Country Music Story*, presented by the North Carolina Arts Council Folklife Section, Spirit Square, North Carolina, Don Reno said: "Snuffy taught me the basic three-finger roll on the five-string banjo when I was just a little boy…That's what turned me on to banjo. Before Snuffy's style, banjo sounded harsh and crude to me."

By this time, there was a group of North Carolina

Vintage Bill Monroe "Hatch" Show Poster. *Courtesy of Pat Ahrens.*

31

bluegrass players who used a three-finger (thumb, index and middle) pattern, or "rolls," which brought out an incredible sound on the banjo. It is DeWitt "Snuffy" Jenkins who is often credited for creating a new voice and a new way of entertaining and experiencing the banjo.

BILL MONROE (1911–1996)

Although not from the Carolinas, William Smith Monroe's influence on the music of the region must be noted. He was born on September 13, 1911, on his family's farm near Rosine, Kentucky. He was the youngest of eight children of James Buchanan "Buck" and Melissa (Vandiver) Monroe, a family of Scottish heritage. Bill grew up in a home filled with music. Birch and Charlie, his brothers, played the fiddle and guitar. Bill played the mandolin, considered a less desirable instrument. Bill Monroe played the flat pick and also incorporated the blues guitar finger-picking style he learned from Arnold Schultz, an African American railroad worker. Like Bill Monroe, many of the musicians credited with early bluegrass acknowledged the contribution of black musicians. The Carter Family and Jimmie Rodgers utilized traditional African American songs, such as "John Henry" and "Sittin' on Top of the World."

Monroe was quoted as saying, "I've always wanted to have some blues in my music." Bill Monroe, like so many renowned bluegrass artists, never learned to read music but learned how to play from those around him.

Bill Monroe's mother died when he was ten, followed by his father six years later. Monroe went to live with his uncle Pendleton Vandiver, a disabled fiddle player. Monroe would travel with his Uncle Pen as the older man entertained at local dances. These special memories inspired one of Bill Monroe's most famous songs, "Uncle Pen," recorded in 1950.

In 1929, a young Bill Monroe moved to Indiana to work at an oil refinery with his brothers Birch and Charlie, along with his childhood friend and guitarist William "Old Hickory" Hardin. Together with Larry Moore, they formed the "Monroe Brothers." The group played for local dances and house parties. Birch Monroe and Larry Moore soon left the group, but Bill and Charlie carried on as a duo, eventually winning spots to perform live on radio stations. They were sponsored by Texas Crystals on several radio broadcasts in numerous states, including South Carolina and North Carolina, from 1934 to 1936.

N. C. BLUE GRASS MUSIC FESTIVAL

CAMP SPRINGS, N. C. CASWELL COUNTY

On State Road 1137 Off Cherry Grove School Road.
Turn At Stokes Butler's House.

AUG. 29-30-31-SEPT. 1

★ IN PERSON ★

- ★ BILL MONROE
- ★ RALPH STANLEY
- ★ MAC WISEMAN
- ★ RED SMILEY
- ★ CLYDE MOODY
- ★ TEX LOGAN
- ★ J. D. CROWE
- ★ RUDY LYLE
- ★ CARL STORY
- ★ GOINS BROTHERS
- ★ RED ALLEN

- ★ OSBORNE BROS.
- ★ JIMMY MARTIN
- ★ RENO & HARRELL
- ★ COUNTRY GENTLEMEN
- ★ LARRY RICHARDSON
- ★ ROGER SPRUNG
- ★ EMERSON & WALDRON
- ★ McCORMICK BROS.
- ★ BLACKWELL & COLLINS
- ★ McCOURY BROS.
- ★ CUT-UPS & ANES

Vintage North Carolina bluegrass festival poster. *Courtesy of Pat Ahrens.*

S. C. Bluegrass Music Festival

Convention Center   Myrtle Beach, S. C.

Fri., Nov. 27 (10 a.m. – 12 p.m.) $4 — Continuous – Sat., Nov. 28 (10 a.m. – 12 p.m.) $5;
Sun., Nov. 29 (10 a.m. – 7 p.m.) $5; SPECIAL 3-DAY TICKET $12; CHILDREN $1 DAILY.

APPEARING FRI., SAT., SUN. — Bill Monroe,
Ralph Stanley, Mac Wiseman, Don Reno-Red
Smiley (together) with Bill Harrell, Carl Story,
Country Gentlemen, Clyde Moody, Chubby
Wise, Charlie Moore, Joe Green, Curley Sechler

APPEARING SAT. & SUN.— Lester Flatt, Jim and
Jessee

APPEARING FRI. & SAT.— Shenandoah Valley
Cut-Ups

...G SUN.— The Lewis Family

...nuffy Jenkins & Pappy

...egrass

BILL MONROE— King Of Bluegrass Nov...
In Country Music Hall of Fame

RE-UNION CONC...

FRIDAY NIGHT— Bill Monroe, Ralph Stanley, Carl Story

SATURDAY NIGHT— Bill Monroe, Clyde Moody, Reno-Smiley

SUNDAY— Lester Flatt, Mac Wiseman, Curley Sechler ALSO Bill Monroe, M... ...eman,
Chubby Wise

CELEBRATE THANKSGIVING WITH THE "GREATS OF BLUEGRASS"— 37 HOURS OF THE
WOR... 'S BEST AND PUREST (NOT ONE SINGLE ELECTRICAL INSTRUMENT WILL BE USED)

...ved Tickets From: Roy Martin, Route 3, Box 341F, Chester, S. C. 29706 Or...

First Myrtle Beach Festival, November 28, 1970. *Courtesy of Pat Ahrens.*

CAROLINA BLUEGRASS

CHARLIE POOLE (1892–1931)

Charlie Clay Poole was born in Randolph County, North Carolina. His parents were Irish immigrants and worked in the textile mill. As a child, Charlie made a banjo gourd and later, with the money he earned as a child laborer in the mill, he purchased his first real banjo for $1.50.

Many claim that an accident he had playing baseball as a boy that partially deformed the fingers on his right hand forced him to play using the three-finger style. When he had saved $200, he purchased a Gibson banjo. Charlie traveled throughout the region playing the banjo and taking odd jobs. By 1920, he was married and settled in Spray, North Carolina. Charlie, Posey Rorer (fiddler) and Norm Woodlieff formed the North Carolina Ramblers. In June 1925, the Ramblers went to New York City for their first recording session. This was at the earliest time of recorded music and only a few records featuring mountain musicians had been released.

The group sang a variety of songs including minstrel songs and traditional ballads. The band also sang burlesque music with risqué lyrics. A 1927 quote in a Columbia record catalogue described Charlie Poole and the North Carolina Ramblers: "Charlie Poole is unquestionably the best known banjo picker and singer in the Carolinas. A dance in North Carolina, Virginia, or Kentucky isn't a dance unless Charlie and the North Carolina Ramblers supply the pep. People everywhere dance all night when these favorites supply the music."

Unfortunately, playing music and dancing were not the only things that kept Poole busy at night. He lived a fast life and drank excessively. His thirst for alcohol is well documented by scholars and by Poole himself through his songs, such as "If the River Was Whiskey," "Take a Drink on Me" and "Goodbye Booze." His drinking increased during the Depression. Nevertheless, by 1931, the North Carolina Ramblers had sold almost one million records. That same year, a Hollywood movie company hired the North Carolina Ramblers to play the music for a western movie to be filmed in California. However, a few weeks before the group was set to leave, Charlie Poole went on a thirteen-week bender to celebrate his good fortune. He suffered a fatal heart attack and died at the early age of thirty-nine.

If the River Was Whiskey
Charlie Poole, 1930 Columbia Records

If the river was whiskey and I was a duck
I'd dive to the bottom and I'd never come up

Oh, tell me how long have I got to wait?
Oh, can I get you now, must I hesitate?

If the river was whiskey and the branch was wine
You would see me in bathing just any old time
Oh, tell me how long have I got to wait?
Oh, can I get you now, must I hesitate?

I was born in England, raised in France
I ordered a suit of clothes and they wouldn't send the pants
Tell me how long have I got to wait?
Oh, can I get you now, must I hesitate?

I was born in Alabama, I's raised in Tennessee
If you don't like my peaches, don't shake on my tree
Oh, tell me how long have I got to wait?
Oh, can I get you now, must I hesitate?

I looked down the road just as far as I could see
A man had my woman and the blues had me
Tell me how long have I got to wait?
Oh, can I get you now, must I hesitate?

I ain't no doctor but the doctor's son
I can do the doct'rin' till the doctor comes
Oh, tell me how long have I got to wait?
Oh, can I get you now, must I hesitate?

Got the hesitation stockings, the hesitation shoes
Believe to my Lord, I've got the hesitation blues
Tell me how long have I got to wait?
Oh, can I get you now, must I hesitate?

EARL SCRUGGS (1924–2012)

Born in North Carolina, Scruggs was raised on a farm in the hamlet of Boiling Springs just outside the town of Shelby. His father, George, a farmer and bookkeeper, also played fiddle and banjo. His mother played the organ and his four siblings played guitar or banjo or both. George Scruggs passed away in 1928, the same year Earl, age four, began playing banjo. By age ten, Earl idolized "Momma" Maybelle Carter and tried to copy her style. He began using his thumb and the two fingers of his right hand to strike the strings. As a teenager, Earl would make the hour or so trip from Flint Hill to Spartanburg to WSPA radio, where he'd watch banjo player Don Reno play live on the air. Between listening and practicing, Scruggs attended the local high school and like most young men in the area, he worked in the Lily textile mill in Shelby, North Carolina, to help support his family. Earl Scruggs continued to practice the banjo, thinking that he must be getting pretty good. In an interview with *The Tennessean*, Scruggs said:

> *Me and Grady Wilkie would sit in the backseat of my '36 Chevy and play music. He'd play guitar and I'd play banjo until they'd motion us to come back into the mill. That's when I finally realized that what I was doing was of interest to other people. They'd stand around and watch us pick. One of them hadn't heard nothing like that before, and he took his hat off, threw it on the ground and said, "Hot damn!" That's the only time I've run into a guy that when he got excited would throw his hat down and dance on it…That's hard on a hat.*

By the time he graduated in 1942, he was ready to set out and make a living as a musician. It didn't take long for him to secure a job playing with the Morris Brothers, a country band who had a radio show at a station in Spartanburg, South Carolina. Other banjo players in North and South Carolina were using the three finger-style, but Earl Scruggs perfected and popularized it.

When he was twenty-one-years old, Bill Monroe invited the talented young banjo player to join Monroe's Blue Grass Boys. The band included Monroe, who sang and played the mandolin; Lester Flatt on guitar; Howard Watts (also known as Cedric Rainwater) on bass; and Chubby Wise on fiddle. Earl performed with the famous bandleader for four years, touring nationally and playing on the Grand Ole Opry in Nashville, Tennessee. Earl earned sixty dollars a week with his "fancy banjo" (Monroe's words) during his Opry debut at the Ryman Auditorium, which made him an instant sensation.

Historians say Earl Scruggs not only popularized the intricate three-fingered style of playing banjo, but Mr. Scruggs both transformed the banjo and inspired nearly every banjo player who followed him. The Gibson Guitar Corporation presented the "Flint Hill Special" banjo to Mr. Scruggs as a gift. He was also honored with the Gibson Lifetime Achievement Award in 2002.

Earl Scruggs Festival, with John Hartford. *Courtesy of Pat Ahrens.*

Foggy Mountain Boys

Earl Scruggs and Lester Flatt are said to have reached their widest audiences with the popular song "Foggy Mountain Breakdown," recorded in 1949 with their group the Foggy Mountain Boys.

The Foggy Mountain Boys are viewed by many as the "landmark band" in bluegrass music. Lester Flatt and Earl Scruggs's Grand Ole Opry show was sponsored by Martha White Flour. Earl Scruggs had already gained recognition for his fast-as-lightning three-finger picking style. This sound was important to the creation of the "high, lonesome sound" associated with Bill Monroe's band. In thinking about the contributions of Earl Scruggs, Ashley Carder, musician and traditional music history enthusiast, said:

> Bluegrass music would not be what it is, or might not even exist, if it had not been for Earl Scruggs. Although there were others playing in a similar style before him and around the same time (Snuffy Jenkins before him, and Don Reno around the same time), Earl brought the three-finger style to front and center in the mid-1940s as a member of Bill Monroe's Blue Grass Boys on the Grand Old Opry. He smoothed out the three-finger style and became very much imitated by other banjo players. From a personal perspective, my first exposure to bluegrass and banjo music was as a very young child, and it was via my dad's 78 rpm record of Earl Scruggs playing his banjo song "Flint Hill Special." That record was played around the house when I was an infant, and I played that record countless times dating as far back as I can remember. I still have this record. We had two record players at home when I was very young. When I was six years old, my grandmother got me my very own record player with ten books of S&H Green Stamps that she had saved from her grocery store purchases. When I became seriously interested in bluegrass music around 1980, it was the Scruggs style of banjo playing that really pulled me into the music. I bought the Earl Scruggs How to Play the 5-String Banjo book and taught myself the Scruggs rolls on the banjo. Nearly every banjo player playing bluegrass music today typically starts with the Scruggs rolls on the banjo.

Homer "Pappy" Sherrill (1915–2001)

Homer Lee Sherrill was born on March 23, 1915, outside Hickory, North Carolina, in the village of Sherrill's Ford, about twenty-five miles north of

Charlotte. As a child, Homer received a tin Sears & Roebuck fiddle for his Christmas gift. It wasn't long before the boy played so well he could draw a large crowd, which greatly pleased his father, especially when they went into town to sell watermelons from the family garden.

Homer was only thirteen when he debuted on WSOC radio (then in Gastonia). In 1934, he also joined the Crazy Water Barn Dance at WBT Charlotte as leader of Homer Sherrill's East Hickory Stringband. The Crazy Water management soon renamed the band the Crazy Hickory Nuts and sent it to WWNC Asheville. When the band dissolved, Sherrill stayed on as fiddler for Bill and Earl Bolick, brothers who gained fame as the Blue Sky Boys. The Blue Sky Boys were another one of great brother acts of the 1930s hillbilly music scene.

Bill and Earl were influenced by the hymns of the Holiness movement growing in the South, as well as folk music and traditional ballads. Both men were born in North Carolina; their parents were "lint heads," a name given to those who worked in the local cotton mills. Bill taught his younger brother to play guitar while he took up the mandolin. Their father loved the emotionally charged hymn singing and steered his sons away from the cotton mills and toward music.

By 1935, Bill Bolick, Homer Sherrill and Asheville native Lute Isenhour had begun to gain a regional following, as did the Crazy Hickory Nuts. The group split following a dispute with the Crazy Water executive, J.W. Fincher. Within months, Bolick and Sherrill were joined by Earl and back in Asheville performing as the Good Coffee Boys, sponsored by JFG Coffee Company. Bill was eighteen and Earl just sixteen years old.

Vintage image of a family baptism. *Courtesy of Louise Wells.*

Vintage North Carolina bluegrass festival poster. *Courtesy of Pat Ahrens.*

In 1938, Homer Sherrill broadcast on WPTF Raleigh with the Smiling Rangers, a band that included Zeke and Wiley Morris and occasionally Wade Mainer. The band split up and Homer retired briefly. In 1939, a top radio announcer named Byron Parker reached out to Homer.

Everyone associated with hillbilly music at that time knew Parker. Byron Parker was also one of the earliest members of the Monroe Brothers band and had been credited with playing a key role in their success as well as the popularization of bluegrass. Parker played with the Monroe Brothers from 1934 to 1937 and played on the group's first recording for Victor in 1936. He left at the same time Bill and Charlie Monroe set out on their separate ways.

Doc Watson (1923–2012)

The Carolina Rebels played with Doc on a few occasions and actually backed him up on a few shows. Doc always impressed me with his skill and his ear—his timing was incredible. But the biggest thing was his down-to-earth attitude and his amazing mind. I had not seen him in probably ten years, and I went to see him the very last time he performed in Newberry [South Carolina]. *I stepped over to him and spoke, and he knew me immediately. We talked about the shows we* [had] *played together. He said he hoped we got the chance to pick together again sometime. Like most of the original "Greats of Bluegrass," I've gotten to meet and know, he was a real person* [who] *made no pretentions and just loved what he did.*
—David Prosser

Arthel Lane "Doc" Watson was born in Deep Gap, North Carolina, in the Blue Ridge Mountains region. He grew up with seven brothers and sisters in a three-room house. Watson went blind before his first birthday from an eye infection. Doc received his first musical instrument, a harmonica, as a Christmas gift at the age of five or six. When Doc was about eleven, his father made him a banjo using the skin of an old dead cat. In a 2012 interview for National Public Radio with Neal Conan, Doc Watson said, "He [Watson's father] brought it to me and put it in my hands, and said, 'Son, I want you to learn to play this thing real well. One of these days we'll get you a better one,' he said. 'Might help you get through the world.'"

Doc worked on the family farm cutting trees, and with the money he earned, he purchased a guitar from a mail-order company. The family home was filled with music; his mother sang old-time ballads at home and everyone sang at the local church. Doc played music on street corners

Jimmie Rodgers, the "Father of Country Music." *Courtesy of Bill's Music Shop and Pickin' Parlor & Willie Wells.*

with his brother in Boone, North Carolina. He would learn the songs he heard on Grand Ole Opry radio broadcasts and was influenced by country music pioneer Jimmie Rodgers.

In 1950, he was touring with a mountain dance band; the group didn't have a fiddle player, so Doc taught himself to play the fiddle part and played it on his guitar.

In 1964, Watson put his own family into the act when his fifteen-year-old son, Merle, joined him as a guitarist. Father and son performed together for twenty years, receiving Grammy Awards for their albums. Merle died in a tractor accident in 1985. Watson, devastated, almost gave up performing. Ashley Carder, member of the band Palmetto Blue and local traditional music history enthusiast, said:

> *Before Doc Watson became more well known in the 1960s, the guitar was primarily a rhythm instrument in bluegrass music. Doc's ability to flat-pick fiddle tunes on the guitar added a new dimension to bluegrass guitar playing and set the stage for others who came after him. I first heard Doc Watson's guitar playing in the late 1970s on a Flatt and Scruggs LP titled* Strictly Instrumental, *which I think originally came out in 1966. I first saw Doc and Merle Watson around 1983 or '84 at Fiddlers Grove near Union Grove, North Carolina.*

Watson's songs echo the Appalachian mountain music of his childhood and captivated audiences around the world. Perhaps Watson's greatest contribution was giving the world a taste of the music and culture of western North Carolina. He revolutionized not just how people play guitar but the way people around the world thought about mountain music.

Roy "Whitey" Grant (1916–2010) and Avral Hogan (1911–2003)

Roy "Whitey" Grant was born in Shelby and Avral Hogan was born in Robbinsville, North Carolina. In 1935, around the time historic Loray Mills was sold to Firestone Mill, the two young men met while working at the mill and began playing together as the Spindle City Boys. Whitey and Hogan made their radio debut on WSPA Spartanburg, and by 1939, they had their show on a new station, WGNC Gastonia. The radio program lasted for fifteen minutes. As soon as they were done, the men ran across town to a large furniture store that hired them to "sit and pick" in the front window while fans gathered to watch. According to the *Old-Time Herald*, Whitey and Hogan were known through church and school performances in the Carolinas and Georgia.

Whitey and Hogan, born with a natural sense of humor, found creative ways to engage their listening audience and "liven" up the shows. They were well known for country and cowboy jokes and songs. Their version of the song "Jesse James," recorded on the Cowboy label, was so popular that they were brought to New York to record on the Decca label and recorded sixteen songs. The duo joined WBT in Charlotte in 1941. Fame followed as a result of their being members of the Briarhoppers group. The show was heard throughout the East Coast. The *Old-Time Herald* noted that during World War II, CBS broadcast the Briarhoppers' show to the armed forces serving around the world.

The Briarhoppers' show ended in 1951, but Whitey and Hogan stayed together, living next door to each other and working together at a post office in Charlotte. In 2003, they were awarded the North Carolina Heritage Award by the North Carolina Arts Council.

Arval Hogan passed away that same year, and Whitey Grant said, "He was closer than a brother. We sang with one voice." Whitey and Hogan performed together for sixty-six years. According to an interview with Joe DePriest for the *Charlotte Observer*, Whitey Grant said, "In those days and in this part of the country, we were as popular as the Beatles. We'd get 12,000 cards and letters a week—some just addressed to Whitey and Hogan."

3
High on the Hog

By 1931, one out of every seven families in North Carolina and one out of every nine families in South Carolina had a radio. In those early days, if you were fortunate enough to have a radio you had it better than a "two biscuit day." Many people might remember this preshow advertisement, which was heard on the popular *Crazy Water Barn Dance* radio show:

> [As a fiddle softly plays in the background, a pleasant and professional male voice delivers a familiar message to the faithful WBT listening audience:]

> *If faulty elimination has given you aching muscles or sore aching joints you call rheumatism, if it is cause to an aggravated condition of arthritis, upset stomach or made your life miserable with backaches or headaches, unstrung nerves or sleeplessness, I honestly believe that I could do you no greater favor, than convince you of the value of Crazy Water Crystals. With this safe, gentle but thorough cleanser, blended by nature, you can relieve faulty elimination—the thing that's probably the cause of your suffering.*

Charles "Crutch" Crutchfield was from Hope, Arkansas, and began his career in radio at station WSPA in Spartanburg in 1929. He had a short stint at WIS in Columbia as announcer before he joined the staff of WBT in Charlotte, North Carolina, in 1933. Crutch was an announcer and advertising salesman and had a reputation for aggressively pursuing

Radio bluegrass musician. *Courtesy of Bill's Music Shop and Pickin' Parlor & Willie Wells.*

sponsors. With the incredible popularity of "old timey" music, Crutch was able to secure new advertisers by promising them an authentic Carolina hillbilly band to promote their products. Business owners jumped at the innovative opportunity. The only problem was Crutchfield didn't have a band. But as they say, "Cain't never did cause cain't never tried."

According to the research of historian and folklorist Dr. Tom Hanchett and documented on the website History South, sponsors sought to sell products such as Peruna tonic, Radio Girl perfume and Kolorbak hair dye. However, the biggest advertiser was Crazy Water Crystals.

> *Announcer: And so the Producers of Crazy Water Crystals, for your pleasure Col. Jack and Shorty's Crazy Hillibillies. Yes, Sir, and here we come with some real "ol timey" mountain music.*

The Crazy Water Crystals Company was located in Mineral Wells, Texas, and became a household word for many rural and working-class Carolinians. Grady Cole "Mr. Dixie," another WBT announcer, would share about the healing powers of "the crystals in the bright green box." Sponsored musical groups included Dick Hartman's Crazy Tennessee Ramblers, Mainer's Crazy Mountaineers, Fisher Hendley and his Carolina Tarheels and Charles Crutchfield's Briarhoppers.

There are many versions of how the name came to be. One story claims that Crutch was on a hunting trip with another WBT announcer, Bill Bivens. The two men were startled when a large rabbit jumped out of a thicket. Bill yelled, "Look at that briarhopper!" The Ramblers band claimed they used "Briarhoppers" as a pseudonym to avoid contractual conflicts. Historians say that the term was also slang for Kentucky migrants at the time. Wherever it came from, Crutch liked the sound, and a North Carolina bluegrass institution was born. According to the Country Music Foundation, the Briahoppers are the longest-running performing act of their kind. Many of the most talented musicians of the era at one time or another played with a member of the Briarhoppers. Original members included Johnny McAllister, Jane Bartlett, Bill Davis, Clarence Etters, Thorpe Westerfield, Homer Drye and Billie Burton.

In 1941, Whitey and Hogan left the Gastonia mill community and moved their families to Charlotte. Whitey and Hogan performed as the featured vocalists with the Briarhoppers until the early 1950s. Crutch was promoted to program director and then station manager, and eventually, he became president of WBT's parent company, Jefferson-Pilot Broadcasting.

During the summer of 1945, WBT introduced a Saturday afternoon barn dance broadcast by the CBS radio network. The show *Carolina Hayride* featured the Briarhoppers along with many fine North Carolina musicians, such as Fred Kirby. Along with the hillybilly music, gospel songs remained popular. Kirby sang about the more serious topics of the time as evident in the lyrics from "When That Hell Bomb Falls."

When That Hell Bomb Falls by Fred Kirby, 1950

Won't you listen my dear brother?
For it's time for us to gather
God is getting mighty angry
For the sinful things we've done
He gave us all this blessed land
And this I cannot understand
A weapon of destruction
To destroy us everyone

Refrain:
When that Hell bomb falls
When that Hell bomb falls
There'll be screaming, dying, praying
When that Hell bomb falls

Yes, it happened in Korea
Where our boys are bravely fighting
Fighting for the peaceful way of life
And our democracy
Have mercy on us Lord I pray
Watch over them both night and day
Keep praying for the whole world
And your help to keep us free
Oh, the fathers and the mothers,
Sisters, wives, and children, brothers
Are still weeping from their losses
In the last war, cold and still
Oh, Lord, please lend a helping hand
We know that You will understand
Save us all these heartaches
If it be Your blessed will

Week after week the radio brought this music to the homes of Carolinians and often ended with the words from a favorite sponsor: "And so friends, if

faulty elimination has caused you to suffer, join the ten million people in America who have tried Crazy mineral water, made from Crazy Water Crystals. It's simple, it's natural. So pucker up and keep smiling."

BRYON PARKER

Bryon Parker organized his first band, the Hillbillies, and soon changed the name to Byron Parker & His Mountaineers. They were also called the Old Hired Hand & His Mountaineers.

These early radio productions were primarily a combination of country music, old time and early bluegrass. In 1939, Parker convinced Homer Sherrill to move his family from Charlotte to Columbia, South Carolina.

The WIS Hillbillies were known for their comedy skits and shows. The group was sought after and played the "kerosene circuit," venues that

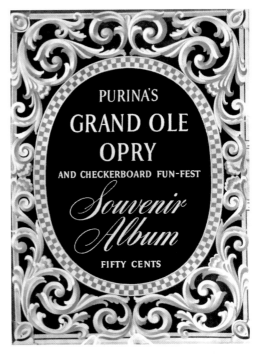

consisted of school auditoriums and courthouse buildings. Snuffy Jenkins wore baggy pants and large shoes and played the washboard. Popular skits included "Hookeyville School" and "Snuffy Cures a Snakebite." Jenkins told Tony Trischka for a "Bluegrass Unlimited" 1977 article: "We didn't even have a P.A. system. We'd play a lot of these little old rabbit school houses down there. Wouldn't hold over a couple of hundred, you know; fifteen and twenty-five cents [admission], and five of us made a living like that. No electricity."

In the 1940s, the group recorded for RCA and DeLuxe Records in Columbia and Capitol Records at the field studios set up by the large recording companies in places such as Charlotte, North Carolina, and Rock Hill, South Carolina. Homer Sherrill became known as "Pappy" when they held an on-air contest to name his second child. The family-friendly nature of the music and entertainment helped pave the way for bluegrass culture. One thing was for sure: the music included the fast three-finger banjo picking of Suffy Jenkins, several years before the style was popularized by Earl Scruggs.

After the death of Bryon Parker in 1948, the group continued on as the Hired Hands. By 1953, the Hired Hands were performing on WIS-TV. They hosted a weekly television show on WIS-TV called *Carolina in the Morning.* Folklorist Mike Seeger recorded Snuffy Jenkins in 1958, and Snuffy continued to be a sought-after folk festival favorite. The Hired Hands found a new audience during the 1960s in folk music revival and began recording while touring festivals across America. They even performed at Carnegie Hall.

Pappy Sherrill received the Carolina Legends Lifetime Achievement Award and is a member of South Carolina Music and Entertainment Hall of Fame.

Snuffy Jenkins retired in the '60s and worked as a car salesman in Columbia, South Carolina.

After almost twenty years, Snuffy Jenkins was honored in his hometown in Rutherford County, North Carolina, with the Snuffy Jenkins Festival. Snuffy and Pappy were also awarded the South Carolina Jean Laney Harris Folk Heritage Award and the North Carolina Order of the Long Leaf Pine.

Opposite, top: The Hired Hands circa 1949. *Left to right, back row*: Tommy Faile (guitar), Ira Dimmery (bass), Homer "Pappy" Sherrill (fiddle) and Marion Kyzer (steel guitar); *front row*: DeWitt "Snuffy" Jenkins (washboard). *Courtesy of Ashley Carder.*

Opposite, bottom: Vintage Crazy Water Crystals and Crazy Barn Dance collection circa 1934. *Courtesy of Pat Ahrens.*

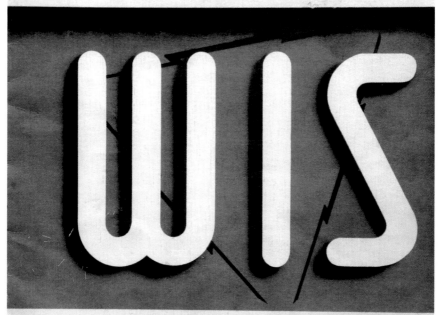

COLUMBIA, SOUTH CAROLINA

WIS

5000 WATTS—560 KC—NBC RED NETWORK

RADIO STATION WIS
COLUMBIA, S. C.

Date _____

As per instructions on the reverse side, I herewith submit all selections contemplated for the _Hired Hand Jamboree_ Program,

to be presented on _Sat._, _Jan 1st 1955_, from _12:00_ P.M. to _12:30_ P.M., originating at _WIS_

Signed: _Jim Hoy_   Address: _____   Telephone No.: _____

1. TITLE OF SELECTION	2. FROM (Production or Suite, etc., if any)	3. MANNER OF PRESENTATION	4. COMPOSER	5. PUBLISHER	6. COPYRIGHT a. Owner	b. Year	Approved by
Theme Song or Signature Music, if any *Bile them Cabbage down*		2IU	Land	Dixie	Bmi		
1 *Orange Blossom Special*		I.	Rouse	Miller	ascap		
2 *What am I Gonna Do about you*		V.	Stone-Chan	Paramount	"		
3 *They're Doing the Mambo*		V.	Raye	V. Monroe	"		
4 *The new Green Light*		V.	Thompson	Brazos Valley	Bmi		
5 *I seen the Rainbow shining*		V.	Edmiston Wright	Stamps-Baxter	Clase		
6 *On the road*		I.	Copt Burland	Stepin Carter	ascap		
7 *Thats alright*		V.	Crudup	Wabash	Bmi		
8 *No more*		V.	Sister	Maple Leaf	"		
9 *Out Behind the Barn*		V.	Bryant	Tannen	"		
10 *Alabama Jubilee*		I	Cobb-Yellen	Remick	ascap		
11							
12							
13							
14							
ALTERNATE NOS. a							
b							
c							

THE HIRED HANDS
Country and Blue Grass Music

PAPPY SHERRILL
Chapin, S.C.
FRANK HARTLEY
Lancaster, S.C.
HAROLD LUCAS
Swansea, S.C.

Hired Hands business card. *Courtesy of Ashley Carder.*

Briarhoppers in the late 1980s. *From left to right*: Hank Warren (fiddle), Shannon Grayson (banjo), Roy "Whitey" Grant (guitar), Arval Hogan (mandolin) and Don White (bass). *Courtesy of Ashley Carder.*

Opposite, top: Vintage WIS program guide circa 1941. *Courtesy of Pat Ahrens.*

Opposite, bottom: Original 1954–55 WIS program logbook, signed by Snuffy Jenkins. *Courtesy of Ashley Carder.*

Prairie Home Companion host, Garrison Keillor, with Homer "Pappy" Sherrill and Rosemary Taylor in back right. *Courtesy of Ashley Carder.*

Flop Eared Mule (Traditional)

Use to have an old banjo,
It was all strung up with twine,
And the only song you could hear me sing was,
I wish that gal was mine.
Well, I wish that gal was mine, boys.
I wish that gal was mine,
And the only song you could hear me sing,
Was I wish that gal was mine.
Whoa mule, you kicking mule,
Whoa mule, I say,
I ain't got time to kiss you now,
My mule has run away.

I HEARD A BANJAR PLAYIN'

THE DARLINGS

I am sure you remember the Darling family—or, as we say it, the Darlins. They lived in a cabin somewhere in the hills just outside the fictitious North Carolina town of Mayberry. Briscoe Darling (played by Denver Pyle) and his five grown children would jump in the old broken-down truck, come to town and seek the assistance of Sheriff Andy Taylor (played by Andy Griffith) when things needed fixin'. The Darling boys were short on conversation but long on talent. Together the members of the family doubled as the show's bluegrass band. In season one, the Darlings sang the show's first song, "Whoa Mule" (or "Kickin' Mule") from inside a homelike cell at the jail. Andy cheerfully played along on his guitar while Aunt Bea bustled about serving beans from a big pot.

In actuality, the Darling boys were part of a professional bluegrass band, the Dillards. The musicians included Doug Dillard (banjo), Rodney Dillard (guitar), Dean Webb (mandolin) and Mitch Jane (bass).

In 2014, the North Carolina Museum of History in Raleigh had the Martin D-28 guitar played by Rodney Dillard on view as part of the exhibit "Carolina Bluegrass: Breakdowns and Revivals." Rodney Dillard's wife, Beverly Cotton-Dillard, a Morrisville, North Carolina native, was also a musician and played the banjo on the television show *Hee Haw*.

The Andy Griffith Show and *The Beverly Hillbillies* might have helped bring bluegrass to the masses, but some Americans naïvely clung to the stereotypical characterization of the bluegrass musician. While the image of the backwoods, unsophisticated hillbilly picking, strumming and singing about moonshine might conjure up images of Appalachia, it was also a popular persona that some musicians found helped endear them to their audiences and lead to commercial success. The audience demand led producers and writers to create television shows that incorporated the music and hillbilly theme. Richard Thompson, a freelance writer specializing in bluegrass music, stated in the January 19, 2013 issue of *Bluegrass Today* that Lester Flatt and Earl Scruggs recorded the "Ballad of Jed Clampett" in January 1963. The song was the No. 1 single on *Billboard*'s Hot Country charts for three weeks and No. 44 on the *Billboard* Hot 100 pop music chart. The "Ballad of Jed Clampett" was used as the theme song for the popular CBS television show *The Beverly Hillbillies*, which ran from 1962 to 1971.

The culture of bluegrass music in North and South Carolina has been and is performed by musicians so skilled that the breakneck speed and tight intricate harmonies seem to be easily achieved. Bluegrass is not simplistic, so don't let the bib overalls fool you.

The Ballad of Jed Clampett by Lester Flatt and Earl Scruggs, 1962

Come and listen to my story 'bout a man named Jed
Poor mountaineer, barely kept his family fed

Daddy John Love played with the Mainer Brothers, J.E. and Wade, on radio station WFNC in the 1930s and '40s. *Courtesy of Ashley Carder.*

"Red" Hutto And The Sand Mountain Boys

Here's another great Blue Grass Band. The Sand Mountain Boys was organized in 1966 and have appeared on various stage shows over the past few years including The Pee Dee Opry in Florence, the Country Music Association Annual Jubilee —1966, 1967, and 1968, and many others — The Ridge Jamboree of course — where they are now regulars. Frank Hutto has done a great job with The Sand Mountain Boys in arranging their tight schedule of show dates.

The Carolina Country Boys

This is our "home-grown" band. The Carolina Country Boys have been playing together for many years so it's just natural that they should be a part of a Ridge Jamboree on the grow.

The 1969 *Ridge Jamboree* on radio station WBLR. The bottom photograph includes Clint Smith on guitar and his young son Steve Smith on banjo. Steve is still playing banjo today in several South Carolina-based bands. *Courtesy of Ashley Carder.*

Next page, top: The Hired Hands' first LP album's reverse image photograph circa 1962. *From left to right*: Julian "Greasy" Medlin, Ira Dimmery, Bill Rea and Homer "Pappy" Sherrill. DeWitt "Snuffy" Jenkins crouches in front.

Next page, bottom: The Dillards, aka "The Darlings," of *The Andy Griffith Show*, with Bill Wells (center). *Courtesy of Bill's Music Shop & Pickin' Parlor.*

Then one day he was shootin' at some food
And up through the ground came a bubbling crude
(Oil, that is, black gold, Texas tea)

First thing you know, old Jed's a millionaire
Kin folks said, "Jed, move away from there"
Said California was the place he ought to be
So they loaded up the truck and they moved to Beverly
(Hills, that is, swimming pools and movie stars)

Well, now it's time to say goodbye to Jed and all his kin
They would like to thank you folks for kindly dropping in
You're all invited back next week to this locality
To have a heaping helping of their hospitality
(Beverly Hillbillies, that's what they call 'em now
Nice folks, Y'all come back now, hear?)

ARTHUR SMITH (1921–2014)

Arthur Smith was born in Clinton, South Carolina, and grew up in Kershaw. His father worked in a cotton mill and also led a brass band. Young Arthur played cornet in his father's band and was already writing his own songs. It wasn't long before Arthur was skillfully playing the guitar, fiddle and mandolin. He loved all types of music including big bands, rhythm and blues, gospel and jazz. The guitarist Django Reinhardt had a great influence on Arthur's musical development and he became well known as a teenager playing on southern radio stations. By the age of fourteen, Arthur had a radio show in Kershaw, and by the time he was fifteen, he had made his first record for RCA Victor.

A musical family, Arthur and his brothers Ralph and Sonny formed a Dixieland jazz band, the Arthur Smith Quartet, and performed frequently on WSPA in the late '30s. The group found that it could gain greater commercial success as a country music band and reinvented itself, according to a 1977 article by Don Rhodes in *Bluegrass Unlimited*. Smith noted:

> *We nearly starved to death until one day we changed our style. We had been*
> *doing a daily radio show in Spartanburg, South Carolina as the Arthur*
> *Smith Quartet. One Friday morning we threw down our trumpet, clarinet*

and trombone and picked up the fiddle, accordion and guitar. The next morning we came back on the radio as Arthur Smith and the Carolina Crackerjacks; my brother Sonny came up with the name. Carolina was because we were from South Carolina and the crackerjack part came from when Sonny found that the word according to the dictionary meant one who is tops in his field.

While serving in the navy in 1947, Arthur recorded "Guitar Boogie." This was his first major hit and had been covered by popular musicians like Les Paul and Chuck Berry. A musician and a scholar, Smith turned down two college football scholarships and an appointment to the Naval Academy to focus on his radio career and starting a family.

In 1941, Arthur married Dorothy Byars; he was now hosting live shows on WSPA Spartanburg, South Carolina. In 1943, they moved to Charlotte, where he frequently filled in with the Briarhoppers and recorded his first record at the Andrew Jackson Hotel in Rock Hill, South Carolina.

In 1944, he rejoined the navy during World War II. After the service, he returned to Charlotte and played guitar with the Briarhoppers and Cecil Campbell's Tennessee Ramblers. In 1947, Arthur Smith and the Crackerjacks signed with MGM Records. By 1948, he had a top-ten country hit with "Banjo Boogie."

In 1955, Arthur Smith recorded the song "Feuding Banjos" with Don Reno. The song became an instant hit on both sides of the pond.

According to the 2014 *New York Times* obituary of Arthur Smith, in Liverpool, England, a relatively unknown young musician struggled with the bass solo in "Guitar Boogie" during his first performance with the band the Quarrymen. The young bass player was Paul McCartney.

By the early '70s, things had begun to heat up even by Carolina standards. The song later became well known worldwide when it was released as "Dueling Banjos," performed by Eric Weissberg and Steve Mandell, from the soundtrack of the movie *Deliverance* in 1972; however, no one gave credit to Arthur "Guitar Boogie" Smith. By 1973, the song had reached No. 2 on the *Billboard* charts, and that's when the real fussin' and fuedin' began. Warner Brothers offered Smith $15,000 as a settlement; Smith chose rather to duel it out and go to trial, where the judge ruled in his favor. Smith recouped all past royalties and future royalties, and the credit was changed to show he had written the song.

From the 1950s to the early 1980s, *The Arthur Smith Show* was seen in eighty-seven television markets, and the famous banjo recording had been used in

The Charlotte Country Music Story (1985), written by George Holt. *Courtesy of Pat Ahrens.*

national commercials by Toyota and Mini Cooper. Once again, the good guy won in the end. His fiddle was also featured in the exhibit "Bluegrass: Breakdowns and Revivals" at the North Carolina Museum of History.

Bill and Harold Lucas, Charlie Johnson and other musicians picking at Bill's Pickin' Parlor. *Courtesy of Willie Wells.*

PART II

STILL PICKIN'
IN CAROLINA

That night [after playing a gig in New York City's Central Park] *we went to a club in Greenwich Village and the bartender recognized us from playing in the park that day. "I want to book you here. You guys are great!" He said. "We want you all to come back up here in two months" I told him, "Back up here?! He said, "You guys are really from South Carolina? I thought that was just an act!"*
—*Ed Dover,* The Drovers Old Time Medicine Show

Nashville is an amazing place but the real music is right here.
—*Jim Graddick*

4

Stories from the Fold

*Bluegrass people—the pickers and the fans—are like one big family. We're all
"folks," and we see ourselves that way. The musicians, by and large, are accessible
and down-to-earth. And the fans are both friendly and caring. We all truly care about
each other, and we know that together we have a very special community, built around
bluegrass music and the good values it represents. I hope that never changes.*
—*Martha Adcock*

Many of the individuals interviewed for this book agreed that they came to music through the family. Children would gather 'round while parents, grandparents, aunts, uncles or other extended family members would play, sing or listen to the music they loved. Be it gospel, old-time or bluegrass music, these children learned how to sing and play in perfect time together, acquired skills and found a place to shine but not at the expense of another. As these children became adults they passed this on to their children and even grandchildren. Some families had their own groups who toured and played together. Others played with different groups or simply together as a family at home. Some folks didn't play at all; the annual festival or weekly bluegrass jams were their chance to reconnect with the spirit of family once again. There is something about bluegrass. Listening to it is like returning to the fold.

*Will the circle be unbroken
By and by, by and by?
Is a better home awaiting
In the sky, in the sky?*

Kristin Scott Benson (age seven) singing with her grandfather Arval Hogan in Gatlinburg, Tennessee, circa 1983. *Courtesy of Kristin Scott Benson.*

Opposite, top: At the home of Bill Wells. *Courtesy of Louise Wells.*

Opposite, bottom: Shirley Carder with the Swinging Countrymen, 1969. *Courtesy of Ashley Carder.*

The Swinging Countrymen

Bill Wells fishing with the family. *Courtesy of Willie Wells.*

CINDY BAUCOM

Most folks who play music had generations before them that did the same. It is more of a "lifestyle" than a hobby.
—Cindy Baucom

Cindy Baucom's father, Jim Brooks, was raised in the northwest corner of North Carolina (Ashe County) and started playing music in his early teens. In later years, he also built instruments. She said:

> Dad had a workshop at the house when he worked on his instruments. I remember the first time he came in with some beautiful wood and said, "This is going to be a banjo," and it became the first of many. For sixteen years, Dad played in a band called the Tarheel Travelers. They would often invite me on stage to sing a song or two. He also played with his brother, Harold, as the Brooks Brothers. Starting in the early 1980s, Mountain Drive was formed with my dad, my uncle, myself and Dean Clawson, a native of Watauga County...and also a very talented luthier and musician. We played mainly in the Southeast...with probably our two "biggest" performances being the 1982 World's Fair in Knoxville, Tennessee, and the

STILL PICKIN' IN CAROLINA

Crosby Celebrity Golf Tournament at the Bermuda Run Country Club, near Winston-Salem, North Carolina.

In 1976, my dad's band played Lester Flatt's Bluegrass Festival in Pinnancle, North Carolina, and that was my first time meeting Mr. Flatt, Jimmy Martin, the Osborne Brothers and Marty Stuart.

Growing up surrounded by the mountains and being exposed to bluegrass music on a daily basis gave Cindy a real love for the genre and allowed her to spend precious quality time with her father. Interesting enough, her first instrument was a piano. When she was eight years old, she started playing piano and saxophone in the school band. By the time Cindy was fourteen, her musical interest had turned to bluegrass and playing rhythm guitar. She was doing it all, including singing by the time she was fifteen. This is when Cindy received her first upright bass, and she realized that was her instrument. Even though she played bluegrass with her father and other regional bands, it didn't take long before she realized that her "true calling" was radio. Cindy said:

> *I started producing and hosting a show on my hometown radio station, WKSK in West Jefferson, North Carolina, after school and on weekends, and I treasure the memory of getting to interview Bill Monroe when I was eighteen years old. That turned into a full-time career in broadcasting. After more than twenty years on local and regional radio stations, I got the opportunity through John Boy & Billy Inc. to put a bluegrass show into national syndication in 2003…and* **Knee-Deep in Bluegrass** *was born.*

Cindy's career includes highlights such as producing the Awards Show for the International Bluegrass Music Association (IBMA) with Earl Scruggs as a special guest. She feels strongly about the IBMA and explained:

> *The International Bluegrass Music Association [IBMA] is a wonderful organization dedicated to furthering careers of bluegrass professionals. IBMA has worked hard for more than twenty-five years to open doors for artists and get the genre of bluegrass recognized on a larger playing field. With programs offered for youth, it keeps the bluegrass format moving forward into the future. Seminars and showcases during the annual convention brings bluegrass professionals, hobbyists and fans together to celebrate the music and learn from one another by networking. Anyone*

serious about their involvement with bluegrass should be a member. More information is available at www.ibma.org.

Cindy has seen how the industry has changed to include traditional, contemporary and progressive bluegrass styles. She hopes that bluegrass will continue to offer something for everyone.

TERRY BAUCOM (IN HIS OWN WORDS)

My parents gave me my first banjo when I was ten years old after I loved the sound of Earl Scruggs's banjo on *The Beverly Hillbillies* theme song. I grew up performing in a local band (The Rocky River Boys) with my father, Lloyd Baucom, and gained other experience around my region with L.W. Lambert & the Blue River Boys and A.L. Wood & the Smokey Ridge Boys. My first professional job (playing fiddle) came in 1970 with Charlie Moore & the Dixie Partners. My first "professional" appearances with Charlie Moore were [at] the Grand Ole Opry and *The Ernest Tubb Midnight Jamboree*. By the mid-'70s, I was one of the founding members of "Boone Creek" with Ricky Skaggs, Jerry Douglas and Wes Golding. In the early part of 1979, Doyle Lawson called to see if I would partner with Lou Reid, Jimmy Haley and himself to form Doyle Lawson and Quicksilver. I was there for the first six years of the band and the first five recording projects. I returned to Quicksilver in 2003 and worked there again for the next four years. Between those stints, I was a founding member of IIIrd Tyme Out, Lou Reid, Terry Baucom & Carolina and BlueRidge.

I toured with the Mashville Brigade in 2010 and played a number of shows with Tony Rice & Mountain Heart. In addition to various band projects I have played on, I recorded my first solo release in 2011 for the John Boy & Billy label called "In a Groove." By 2013, the second project for the label was released, "Never Thought of Looking Back." The single "What'll I Do" from that recording was awarded IBMA Recorded Event of the Year for 2013 and was the most played song on radio, according to *Bluegrass Today*. In the fall of 2013, after being a "sideman" for four decades, I formed my own band, Terry Baucom's Dukes of Drive.

It is a wonderful life traveling the world and sharing the music with friends. I have enjoyed a lot of highlights throughout but am very proud of an instrumental I wrote called "Knee-Deep in Bluegrass," which was the title cut of a recording for Rebel Records that picked up the award for Recorded

Cindy and Terry Baucom. Mike Lane Photography. *Courtesy of Cindy Baucom.*

Event of the Year from the IBMA in 2001. This song became the theme song for my wife's syndicated radio show, *Knee-Deep in Bluegrass.* Sharing the music and its experiences with your spouse is a great thing. When you understand each other's passion for the music, life is harmonious all the way around!

Both Terry and Cindy are inductees to the Blue Ridge Music Hall of Fame and continue to be one of the Carolinas' most well loved and respected bluegrass couples.

Kristin Scott Benson

Kristin said her memory might be a little fuzzy, but she believes she was about five years old when she stepped on the stage in Gatlinburg, Tennessee, to perform with her grandfather Avral Hogan and his partner Roy "Whitey" Grant; even a fuzzy recollection can create a powerful memory.

When I spoke with Kristin, she reminisced about the trip and explained how Whitey drove, her "Paw-Paw" sat in the front seat and she rode in the back with her "Me-Maw" Evelyn and Polly, Whitey's wife. It was a long trip. Kristin spent the majority of the time with her head on Me-Maw's lap. She, of course, had brought along her little mandolin. It was the perfect-sized instrument at the time for a little girl with mighty big dreams.

Growing up in Union, South Carolina, her mother's daddy, Arval Hogan, was a member of the old-time duo Whitey & Hogan and the Briarhoppers. In the 1930s and 1940s, the North Carolina–based duo had made significant contributions to the music industry. Kristin grew up surrounded by music;

Kristin Scott Benson at six years old. *Courtesy of Kristin Scott Benson.*

Avral Hogan played the mandolin and her father, Fred, played the banjo.

Perhaps the best way parents can support children is to expose them to as much beauty and positive influences as they can as early and as often as possible. You never know what will capture the young imagination or plant the seeds that will last a lifetime. Kristin was nine years old when her folks took a family trip to a bluegrass festival in Dahlonega, Georgia. When she saw Doyle Lawson and Quicksilver with Scott Vestal on banjo perform, it literally set the path from which she never strayed. In a 2010 interview with

72

Tim Kimzey, she stated, "That was the first year I could really remember bluegrass impacting me. When I saw that band it floored me, and my favorite thing about it was the banjo." Not long after the festival, her parents gave her a banjo as a present. A few months later there was a fire that destroyed the family home, leaving one wall standing; everything was lost, including her precious banjo.

When she was thirteen, she received a banjo from her parents as a Christmas gift. She said, "I took lessons in Greenville, about a ninety-minute drive from home." Kristin was involved in softball and basketball. She was also in the marching band, where she played trombone. That was before the banjo took over her life. She said, "I was even playing banjo before I went to school in the morning. We had a pool table, and I kept my banjo on the pool table out of the case. Every time I went by it, I would play some."

In 1989, Kristin was a member of a gospel band and performed with the all-girl Nashville semiprofessional group Petticoat Junction. She was so busy playing music that she missed her senior prom. Kristin's parents were always supportive, but she knows now how worried they must have been when she was traveling by herself at such an early age. After high school, Kristin attended Belmont University in Nashville and continued to play with a variety of bands the entire time. She was a student and a working musician. According to a 2010 interview with Larry Nager, a Nashville-based writer, documentary filmmaker and musician, by her sophomore year, she was playing with the Larry Stephenson Band (LSB), and she was on the road almost every weekend. She said, "For me to get to join that band at nineteen years old, that was really when I got the feel of playing in a band that was busy. We played ninety shows a year, and that was invaluable. You can practice and you should practice alone, but experience in a band setting is crucial. And that's when I really developed into a true band player." She was meeting musicians from around the country. Though they had met before, Kristin and Wayne Benson didn't begin dating until they performed at a bluegrass festival in Florida in the late '90s. They married three years later in 2000.

After college, she stayed in Nashville. Her career took off, and she had powerful mentors along the way. Benson became friends with bluegrass legend Sonny Osborne. The Osborne Brothers had also mentored and befriended many of the members of the Grascals. When the band was searching to fill an open spot, Sonny Osborne recommended Kristin, and she became a Grascal in 2008.

This was a continuation of good news. In October 2006, John Lawless with *Bluegrass Today* shared this announcement:

We just received news of the arrival of Hogan Wayne Benson, who was born on October 6, 2006. His parents are Kristin Scott Benson, banjo picker with Larry Cordle & Lonesome, Standard Time, and Wayne Benson, mandolinist with The John Cowan Band…If ever a child was born with an impeccable bluegrass pedigree, young Hogan may be the one. Our most sincere congratulations go out to Kristin and Wayne, who we trust will be as exceptional as parents as they have been on stage and in the studio.

A year after the birth of their son, Kristin and Wayne moved to Boiling Springs, South Carolina, to be closer to her parents. The baby, Hogan, now had his grandparents to help care for him when Kristin and Wayne were busy on the road, recording or promoting their music.

In 2008, Kristin recalls a major media event that required a photo shoot for a new Grascals album entitled *The Famous Lefty Flynn's* on Rounder Records. The band members rode in a large bus with a crew consisting of about six makeup, costume and production staff. This was the big leagues. They would stop at various locations and pose while the camera and crew buzzed about. Pictures were taken at a trendy restaurant in downtown Nashville, a southern mansion in the country and various scenic outdoor locations. Kristin recalls they were sitting on the bus while the photographer

The Grascals, Keoni K. Photography. *Courtesy of Kristin Scott Benson.*

was frantically working to set up the next shot. She said, "I'm not sure who it was, but someone asked me, 'So Kristin [gesturing to the bus and crew] what do you think, huh?'" Kristin remembers looking out the window, watching the photographer adjusting the lights to get that perfect outdoor look and answering, "I think this isn't why I started playing the banjo, but I'm still thankful for the opportunity to be here."

Kristin Scott Benson has attained a national identity as one of the top bluegrass banjo players on the scene and has been featured with cover stories in *Bluegrass Now*, *Bluegrass Unlimited* and *Banjo Newsletter*. Kristin is also a four-time winner of "Banjo Player of the Year" from the International Bluegrass Music Association.

WAYNE BENSON

People [who] *play music for the joy, or for the fact that they truly want to learn, or the artsy side or it, that you really want to do something that is creative, or do something that's your own. Those are all great reasons to be motivated to play, not talking to someone and saying, let's come up with a hook line so we can sell fourteen million copies of this record. That's what corrupts this whole experience.*
—*Wayne Benson*

From the time Wayne Benson was five or six, until the time he was fifteen or sixteen, his father, John Benson, played music with his uncles. The family members would gather together and share a meal, music and stories. Wayne would join them playing the guitar and mandolin. Wayne said:

> *I certainly wasn't growing up in 1930 or the 1940s, but the tradition wasn't actually that far removed. We were poor people. We moved the table to one side of the kitchen and got all the chairs out so people would have a place to sit down. No one danced; it wasn't like a shindig. All the men gathered in the kitchen and played music and all the women gathered in the den. Many, many pots of coffee* [were drunk], *and my mom would have maybe a homemade cake, and that is what we did. It was a fairly inexpensive way to be entertained. It wasn't like it was the only way for us to hear music, like in the '30s when they didn't have a radio. But for us it was a really cool way to visit as a family, so there was a lot of that kind of tradition. Bill Monroe songs, Flatt and Scruggs, Osborne Brothers,*

Jimmy Martin the Country Gentlemen. My parents were cool people even though they weren't artsy people, they weren't educated people...they knew that playing a musical instrument was a healthy thing for someone to do.

This sounds like a story straight from a farmhouse or mountain cabin, but that was not the case at all. Wayne grew up in Concord, North Carolina, just outside Charlotte. There was a busy highway a few blocks from the house and the large shopping mall less than a mile away. The fact that Wayne did not grow up in the mountains or on a farm made no difference at all. He said, "It was a part of the tradition. You know, it goes far beyond the music itself. It was tradition for us. Like around Christmas when everyone really steps up and makes a special effort to make time for family and do more of that kind of thing. Playing music was part of it."

Even in the town of Concord, the music preferred by the Benson family was just plain "mountain." Wayne would ride his bicycle to the music store at the shopping plaza, where he would buy the music of Ricky Skaggs and the band Boone Creek. He shared the story of how he received his first instrument: "I had a mandolin at the house, somebody owed my dad money, I think twenty bucks or something, and they didn't have the money to pay him, and they had an old mandolin. I think they had gotten the thing out of an old Sears and Roebuck catalogue!"

Music was important to Wayne's father, John, for many reasons. It wasn't just a nicety; it was a necessity: "My dad played the fiddle and banjo; it was as much as a therapy for him as it was about music. He had a construction business, and pressure and deadlines and stuff like that to worry about."

Because of his father's relationship to the music he loved, Wayne made some decisions at a young age about how he believed a musician should approach his craft. He said:

You want to be a more efficient player and you want your musicianship to grow, but at the same time, it's supposed to be fun and it's supposed to help take your mind away from all those things. This book is going to provide that therapy for people. I remember my dad getting in the pickup truck he owned and turning the radio on, and Barbara Mandrell was on the radio. It was that age of the really slick stuff, with orchestra in the background and all that and I remember my dad saying, "Man music is getting so bad you can't even listen to it anymore." And he would try to find like Buck Owens or Merle Haggard or something like that [that] he identified with. The realness of it, songs like the ones we would play sitting around the kitchen, that it was real you know?

STILL PICKIN' IN CAROLINA

Wayne shared a comical story about how he learned to drive. He needed to learn to drive if he was going to get together with the other boys his age; all of them were anxious to try their hand at playing the more contemporary bluegrass songs. Wayne found a creative way to practice driving before he had a license. His father had a 1969 Chevrolet short-bed truck with a 250-cubic-inch straight-six engine, which he used for his construction business. Wayne needed to learn how to operate the clutch so he could get his driver's license. So he developed a plan. He would tell his father that he was going to go out to wash the truck tires. His method of washing the tires was to move the vehicle, rather than the bucket and hose. When one side was washed he would get in the truck, back it out the driveway and turn it around so he could wash the other side. When it was time to rinse the tires, back in the truck he would go.

It worked. He learned how to stop, start and shift gears on the old green truck; he was able to get his license and start jamming with his friends; and the old work truck had some mighty clean tires.

During these late-night jams, Wayne and Clay Jones, a fellow picking partner, explored the newgrass style as well as the specific techniques of mandolinist Sam Bush.

Wayne was drawn to the sound of the mandolin in the '70s. Once, his father purchased a quality mandolin and used a little reverse psychology by instructing Wayne not to touch it. Well, Wayne has been attached to the instrument ever since. Wayne said:

> *Terry Baucom, he's a North Carolina guy and a huge part of what I associate with the modern sound of bluegrass of the Carolinas. Wes Golden on guitar, Terry Baucom on banjo, Steve Bryant on electric bass, Jerry Douglas on Dobro®, they were really plowing the trail for contemporary music. I picked that Boone Creek record up. I wasn't old enough to drive a car yet, but I was doing yard work and stuff over the summer to earn extra money. I would buy these records at a local music store and also bought Quick Silver Rides Again; also the JD Crowe album 0044, which is the only record I'm aware of people can refer to by the catalogue number. When it comes to being influential on bluegrass? That one is leader of the pack!*

There were traditional bluegrass festivals and then there were the "hippie" festivals. Wayne described them:

> *Then there were the hippie festivals, the audience for the more contemporary music…from a musician's standpoint, bluegrass can be such a music of*

execution, it's all about your timing, tone, fundamentals. Your musicianship can be totally measured by your ability to do those things. But the bands at the hippie fest are approaching it as what can we do that's creative. The coolest thing about newgrass is that the integrity and the tone never suffered because they were trying to do something creative. They were still solid musically when they played. When you are talking about the tradition and the different ways people approach bluegrass. The style you are going to play is based on tradition and other things you heard and, are you really going to try and put your stamp on it?

A career in music, he said, "kind of crept up on me." He was working for his father's construction business and performing with the band Livewire. His father liked the fact that Wayne was making music, so whenever he needed time off to perform, his father made sure he had it.

It was a real commitment for everyone in his first professional band. Wayne lived in North Carolina, another band member lived in Atlanta, one lived on Long Island in New York and the last lived in West Virginia. It cost the young men a fortune to get together and play, but they did it. They recorded for Rounder Records, one of the largest independent labels in the world. Livewire was creative; the group played newgrass music and would plug instruments in on stage. Wayne Benson was not trying to please anyone; he was finding his way as a musician at nineteen years old. He said, "I was just doing my thing."

Wayne worked with Livewire for three years. In 1992, he joined the critically acclaimed Atlanta-based band IIIrd Tyme Out. He has been featured on the cover of *Bluegrass Now, Mandolin Quarterly* and *Bluegrass Unlimited* and has received numerous awards from the IBMA, as well as the Society for the Preservation of Bluegrass Music of America (SPBGMA) Mandolin Player of the Year Award for five consecutive years. In 2003, he released his first solo project, an instrumental anthology, and also that year, Gibson joined forces with Benson to create the Wayne Benson Signature mandolin. With all his awards and endorsements, Wayne continues to believe that integrity, devotion to his family and excellence in his craft are a top priority. On our phone call interview, the family was headed out for the weekend: "Kristin and I are going to take our little boy and head down below Greenville into the southern part of the state, for a fishing trip is what we have going on. This has been almost like a vacation week for us…we just love it when we all are home together."

Above: Wayne Benson with his father, John. *Courtesy of Kristin Scott Benson.*

Right: Wayne Benson. *Courtesy of Kristin Scott Benson.*

CAROLINA BLUEGRASS

LUCAS FAMILY

[Bluegrass is] *gonna be a lot different twenty years from now, it keeps on what's the word? Progressing. The young kids are picking it up. I seen them on television and they are real good, playing fiddle, guitars and banjo. But some of the old-time bluegrass songs like "John Henry," I hope they stay around forever.*
—Harold Lucas

It would be mighty chancey to find a time when someone from the Lucas family of Calhoun and Lexington Counties did not play some type of string instrument. In fact, I'd rather jump barefoot off a six-foot stepladder into a five-gallon bucket full of porcupines than waste my time even tryin'.

You will want to hold on to your hat because the Lucas music playin' family tree will have your head spinning faster than Earl Scruggs playin' his lightning fast banjo tune "Randy Lynn Rag." In order to try to get the dates and names correct of the long line of "this one begat that one, begat this one" linage, a call to the home of Annette and Harold Lucas was required.

The phone rang (*ring, ring*), and then I heard a *click*. I thought I must have dialed the wrong number, so I tried it again. Once again, the phone sounded, *ring, ring*, and suddenly, a stern voice on the other end said, "I don't take calls from any so-lis-it-TORS!" And once again, *CLICK*. No, this was definitely not an answering machine, so I tried the number again, and this time, I was ready. As soon as the phone stopped ringing, I raced into my introduction, "I'm not a solicitor. I'm a friend of Pat Ahrens. Randy said I could call." There was a pause on the line. Annette Lucas responded, "Oh, well why didn't you say that the first time?" She was busy this particular morning making cake and fixing breakfast at the same time. Although she assured me that she had the Lucas family bluegrass history written down, I would be better off speaking to her husband, Harold. She said, "Talk to him. He's better at remembering, and besides, he's right here. He just got up cuz he knows I'm making a cake."

Harold Lucas was happy to provide the missing information and Annette, although she was busy in the kitchen, could be heard adding her own bits and pieces of information as we went along.

Charlie Daniel Lucas (1879–1962) was born in Lexington County. He was a fiddle player and passed music down to Claude Sr., Lester, Otis, Jerod and C.D. All the boys were musical. Harold started playing the banjo when he was six years old. He explained how his daddy bought him a banjo for $2.50 in the early 1930s. He said, "My daddy would put me on his knee and showed me how to use my fingers." Harold met his wife, Annette, at church, and they both loved the song "Randy Lynn Rag." Living in Nashville, Harold got to see Earl Scruggs and Lester Flatt play at the Opry. Their son was born in Nashville on the same day as the great Bill Monroe, and they decided to name him Randy in honor of their favorite song. Harold served in the Vietnam War and played music for the troops. Annette was

The Lucas And Harmon Brothers

Well what can we say? Space is just too limited to say it all when it comes to The Lucas And Harmon Brothers. They are one of the most popular groups ever to appear on the big stage. These brothers have stood by the Jamboree through thick and thin. Blue Grass seems not to be accepted as it once was — but there's no truth to this when it comes to The Lucas And Harmon Brothers. These guys are showmen. They enjoy playing and performing about ten times better than anybody else. They're always up to a good time and the audience just loves 'um.

Very busy describes The Lucas And Harmon Brothers best. Show dates all the time. Charity work is very big with these boys. They're always ready to help a church or organization do something good. Of course their regular appearances number very high — and if there's a contest to be won these natural born musicians are off to get the prize. Everybody loves The Lucas And Harmon Brothers — and they love the people. Never fail to see them if you can.

The Lucas and Harmon Brothers on the WBLR *Ridge Jamoree*, circa 1969. *Courtesy of Ashley Carder.*

from South Carolina, so they left Tennessee so she could be closer to home. Harold loved everything about Nashville and the Grand Ole Opry. He said, "I would have stayed up there when I got out of the service, but my wife wanted to go home." There was a music scene in the Carolinas and Harold quickly became an important part of it. He said, "WIS had a radio program from 12:00 to 12:30, and you know what they say?" The eighty-seven-year old bluegrass master chuckled, "The best fiddle players might come out of North Carolina, but the best banjo players come out of South Carolina!"

Harold remembers attending the Union Grove Fiddlers Convention in the 1950s. He loved hearing the Stanley Brothers with their beautiful harmonies in the old mountain style. His favorite song is "John Henry," the steel-driving man. According to Harold, that is the song he first taught Randy to play when he was about nine or ten years old. Harold was performing regularly with his brothers and the Claude Lucas band. In 1971, he was performing with the Hired Hands, and it wouldn't be long before his banjo-playing youngest son, Randy Lucas, would be joining them.

RANDY LUCAS

My dad [Harold] had a banjo and guitar. We had a bass fiddle. I don't know why I picked it up. Somebody must have put it in my hands. I learned to play a little bit, songs like John Henry and Cripple Creek. We also had a big old acoustic upright bass. I would play it at church and I had to stand on a chair because it was so big.
—Randy Lucas

Randy Lucas was always attracted to the sound of the banjo. Although he did a little playing when he was five, he put it down for several years. He could also play the bass fiddle by the time he was eight or nine. Not only could Randy play a variety of instruments, but he could also Buck dance. Buck dancing is a folk dance largely associated with the North Carolina Piedmont region. The family would go to the town of Maggie Valley, where there were always events and festivals going on (and where there was a general store at which Randy often performed), because his father played there with the Lucas Brothers band.

Harold and Annette decided to let Randy dance on the porch of the General Store for the tourists. Randy recalls how his parents would dress him in a pair of overalls and put a hat on his head. People would come up to the porch while his father would play music and Randy would dance. Once during a three-day festival, the little boy made $133.

However, by the time he was ten years old, Randy was playing the banjo on a regular basis. I guess he hung up his dancing shoes because he has been playing bluegrass music ever since.

Perhaps simply living in the Lucas home predestines one to have a musical ear. Randy shared that even the family pets were highly skilled as far as pets go. They had parakeets that learned to talk, and there was one hunting dog, a black-and-tan coon dog, about which Randy said, "We could have won trophies with the dog. That dog would almost talk to you. We would take him hunting down at Saylor Lake [the natural oxbow lake close to where his mom and dad still live], and he learned to tree squirrels. He was a silent trailer and would only bark if there was a 'coon in a tree. That dog was so smart he had a different bark for coon and a different bark for a 'possum. He was right almost every time. My father was really attached to that dog."

While attending Calhoun Academy in St. Matthews, Randy, like most teenagers, listened to rock-and-roll. He found ways to incorporate the new popular musical sounds with his traditional bluegrass. He believes he wrote his first song when he was fifteen or sixteen. Although he doesn't remember what the lyrics were about, he said, "It was probably about girls."

Randy found a way to blend the popular music of the day to create his own unique bluegrass banjo sound. Randy remembers one of his first girlfriends was a young lady he met as a teenager while the family was attending the Snuffy Jenkins Festival in North Carolina. Her name was Valerie, and her family made the trip to North Carolina from Florida to hear the music. Randy didn't have a driver's license at the time, but somehow, he managed to get hold of a car. Valerie was so incredibly impressed and invited him to visit her family in Florida. Randy never made the trip to visit his bluegrass festival sweetheart, but he admitted that he still has a few of the old love letters stashed away someplace.

Randy was serious about playing the banjo, and in 1995 at the suggestion of a friend, he took his first solo trip to Winfield Kansas to compete in the National Bluegrass Banjo Championships. Randy came in third that year. In 1996, he came in second, and in 1997, he won the first-place prize. He said, "Winfield, they give away some really nice banjos!" Randy has gone on to win numerous banjo championships, including first place at Merle Fest in Wilksboro North Carolina, when he was thirty-four years old. Randy enjoys the challenge of competing and growing as a musician.

CAROLINA BLUEGRASS

Randy has a great deal of energy as well as a sense of humor. Growing up in such a prominent bluegrass family, you would think Randy would have been prepared for anything. He admits, however, that the one thing he didn't know was how many banjo jokes he would have to endure over the years.

> *Question: What's the difference between the banjo and an onion?*
> *Answer: Nobody cries when you cut up the banjo.*

And the one he first heard from his mandolin-fiddle musician friend, Danny Harlow.

> *Question: What do you call a pretty girl on a banjo player's arm?*
> *Answer: A tattoo!*

South Carolina bluegrass historian Pat Ahrens has written six feature articles on Randy Lucas and the Lucas bluegrass dynasty. Her articles have been published in *Bluegrass Unlimited* (1989) and the *Banjo Newsletter* (1997). Her article about Randy Lucas entitled "A Magnetic Musician" was published in 1996.

Randy met his wife, Dee, at Bill's Music Shop & Pickin' Parlor. It was right around the time he had graduated from Bible College in Columbia. It was obvious the young woman could play bluegrass because she was holding a guitar. The only thing he could think of to say was "Can you dance?" The couple found that they had many things in common and continued to go to Bill's on Friday nights.

Randy's daughter, Alison Bailee Lucas, is named after Alison Krauss. Randy and Dee have always been fans of the talented singer, and Randy had the opportunity to play on stage with her once. When reflecting on the Lucas family legacy, Bailee said:

> *I think there are a good many people who are familiar with bluegrass who hold the Lucas name highly when it comes to bluegrass music. Although my dad certainly hasn't made himself as public as he could and hasn't really made any CDs, he's fairly well known in the bluegrass world. And the fact that my granddad [Harold Lucas] was able to play with Greasy, Snuffy Jenkins, Pappy Sherrill as part of the Hired Hands is just amazing to me as they were such an influential part of the growth of bluegrass. But outside the world of bluegrass, not many people know or appreciate these musicians and the bluegrass world is not very big in comparison to many*

others. The traditions still carry on though. There is a little sign at Bills, where my granddaddy always used to play during the jams after open stage, with a hat that my granddaddy cut holes into that still hangs on a wall, and in little ways like that, I think the Lucas name will carry on for a while.

Bailee demonstrated an aptitude for music as a young child and studied the Suzuki method for violin. Bailee, now a senior at the University of South Carolina, continues to play; however, she has many other interests as well. When it comes to bluegrass, Bailee said:

I think the most surprising thing I've seen with bluegrass as I've grown and explored other types of music is the amount of talent it takes to play it well. Many people have an idea of bluegrass as being an old, irrelevant kind of music that is just people framming away at banjos and fiddles and while that is sometimes the case unfortunately, true bluegrass is so much more! Lyrically, it tells stories of hardship and the good old days or sometimes is a silly song about animals or can even morph into dark songs about murder. It really captures a picture of life as it used to be that just doesn't really exist anymore and I love that a lot of memories are preserved in song this way. Musically, bluegrass takes a surprising amount of talent! It is relatively easy to play but to play it well takes many, many years of practice and requires you to be exposed to other musicians to really grow. The improvisation that is required when a musician takes a break really is an art form and again takes years of practice to master and this is one reason why I love bluegrass so much. On the other hand, I also just love that bluegrass musicians are so welcoming to others and the whole idea of a "jam-session" really embodies the idea of a community coming together to share musical ideas with one another which help inspire, teach and grow one another.

Randy Lucas is a minister at Salem Baptist Church in North, South Carolina, and has incorporated his love of music into his ministry. Every fifth Sunday, the church has a bluegrass-Gospel service. Randy still loves the traditional hymns; "Blessed Assurance" and "Rock of Ages" are his favorites.

Randy believes twenty years from now the banjo, guitar, mandolin, fiddle and bass will be popular but that the young musicians might not be as tied to the traditional elements that have given bluegrass music its identity.

In a 2014 interview with Hastings Hensel, Randy described the philosophy behind his band, the Randy Lucas Trio, saying, "Some bands you listen to are

Randy Lucas, circa the late 1970s or early 1980s. *Courtesy of Pat Ahrens.*

purist. They want to have that high, lonesome sound. But many of the bands today are like me. We've heard all kinds of stuff. So when we play, you can call it bluegrass, but some of it's more high energy."

Randy is as open to new ideas and creativity today as he was as a teenager. He said:

> *I am not so much about retaining a certain sound as much as playing something that is creative and musical. When Beethoven, Mozart, Bach created music it seems that it was something that was not retained from something in the past as it was new and fresh. It seems there is a lot*

of influence that comes to every musician, but I feel that music should be as creative and individual as people are and go as far as their unique personalities will take it.

BILL WELLS (1927–2011)

Few people have had the positive impact on the bluegrass music scene in this state that Bill Wells has. Celebrating over two decades of managing his music store in 2007, Bill almost single-handedly gave the music a home.
—Pat Ahrens

Bill grew up in southwestern Virginia and lived in the same general vicinity as industry giants like the Carter family and the Stanley Brothers. Bill's family were neighbors of the Carter family, and the children went to school together. After school, the children would all gather at the store owned by AP Carter. It was in this space that young Bill Wells heard and learned to play music from many of the finest great musicians around. According to Pat Ahrens, noted South Carolina historian, author and longtime family friend, when Bill's family would go to town to shop on Saturday morning, the boy had a habit of trailing behind musicians who played on the streets. Bill's first instrument was a harmonica, which he purchased from a mail-order catalogue.

Early in his career, he played with a gospel quartet while being mentored by experienced musicians he would meet at WCYB Radio Station in Bristol, Virginia. During World War II, Bill joined the navy and purchased his first guitar with his pay. Bill met his wife, Louise, and the couple had their first date while he was in Charleston. As they say, the rest is history.

After his navy career ended, Bill started his own band, Bill Wells and the Blue Ridge Mountain Grass, in the early 1970s. Bill brought his family to Columbia, South Carolina, in 1984 and was one of the founding members and the first president of the South Carolina Bluegrass and Traditional Music Association. Bill also became a member of IBA (International Bluegrass Association) in 1985.

Bill loved bluegrass, and there was no place he would rather be than with his musician friends. He wanted to open a music store, not just another store that sold merchandise to customers, but he wanted something different. According to Pat Ahrens, he wanted to create a unique place where musicians could come and play, socialize and work on their music together,

Above: Bill and Louise Wells on their first date. *Courtesy of Louise Wells.*

Left: Bill and Louise Wells with their children, Willie and Mike. *Courtesy of Louise Wells.*

like a family. His first store was on State Street, but it didn't take long for them to outgrow it. Musicians came from near and far; this was exactly what they had been waiting for. Bill and Louise opened Bill's Music Shop & Pickin' Parlor on Meeting Street in West Columbia. In addition to operating the business, Bill continued to be lead singer and rhythm guitarist for the Blue Ridge Mountain Grass.

Pickers would gather around and have, as Pat Ahrens calls them, "musician meetings on Meeting." The music hall behind the store boasted concerts that would attract well-known performers. He was a visionary and the first person in South Carolina committed to making professional musicians accessible to their local fans. Bill Wells encouraged many budding musicians. Some of them, like Jim Graddick, were children at the time. Jim stated:

> *My first encounter with Bill probably happened the first time I ever went to Bill's* [Pickin' Parlor]. *He used to stand over by the side of the stage and listen to the open stage all evening. He made it a point to meet me and encouraged me to "keep on playing" as most twelve-year-olds were giving up music for football or skateboards. I remember one night I needed some cork to go under my chinrest (call it a fiddle malfunction). I couldn't play without it. I asked Bill if I could buy some, and he peeled some off and gave it to me. I had never been given anything for free in a store, but every time I tried to buy something little, he would just give it to me. I still have the cleaning rag, polish and a ukulele pick that he gave me between 2002 and 2005. It seems small, but it was a huge gesture to me. Especially since he never gave anything away!*

No matter how many big names came to town, a favorite band was always Bill Wells and his Blue Ridge Mountain Grass. The Blue Ridge Mountain Grass consisted of many fine musicians from the area, and for many of them, performing with Bill Wells remains one of the brightest memories they have. That is certainly how Ashley Carder feels.

> *Bill Wells was like a bluegrass daddy to me. I met Bill in the late 1980s and started going to his Pickin' Parlor right after he opened it. I met so many musicians at Bill's and made so many music friends. Bill was from the hills of Virginia and grew up not far from Ralph Stanley and the Carter Family. Actually, the Carters were some kind of cousins of his. Bill loved bluegrass music and probably did more to promote the music than anyone around the Midlands of South Carolina from the 1990s to 2010 time frame. Bill*

was a stickler for tradition and would not allow electric instruments in his Friday night open stage and jam sessions. He liked the early bluegrass styles of Monroe and Flatt & Scruggs and the Stanleys, and he loved to play their music. I started playing in Bill's band around 1990 or 1991 and played with him off and on for over twenty years, right up until his death. Due to my work and my family, I could not always be committed to his band as much as he would like, so he had other long-term fiddlers over the years, including Lewis Price, Willis McMillan, and others. Lewis played fiddle with him a lot and was his main fiddler for many years, but sometimes Lewis wouldn't be able to play for extended periods and I would be his fiddler.

Bill took me to Carter Fold in Virginia several times, and it was always fun to play there. The people there liked Bill and they really seemed to like my fiddle hoedowns. Bill was planning another trip up there the year he died, and he asked me to go with him. After he found out that he had cancer and was sick, he pulled me aside one night at his Pickin' Parlor and put his arm around me and told me, "I guess we won't get to go to Carter Fold like I told you. I'm too weak to go," and he started crying. I cried too and hugged him. He passed away a month or two later, and I played the fiddle at his funeral service and at the visitation. I played at a lot of good gigs

Bill Wells and the Blue Ridge Mountain Grass. *Courtesy of Louise Wells.*

Bill Wells (left) with Bill Monroe (right), the "Father of Bluegrass Music," circa the late 1970s. *Courtesy of Ashley Carder.*

when I was with Bill's band. We played for several governors, lieutenant governors and business people from the Chinese Cotton Growers in China, the Columbia Museum of Art, the South Carolina State Museum and so many other jobs. Bill was always good to me and was a good guy to work for. He was always promoting bluegrass music in the community and was a great ambassador for the music. I miss him. The bluegrass scene in the Columbia area would not be what it is today had it not been for Bill Wells and his Pickin' Parlor.

Bill Wells received numerous honors and awards through the years. In 1984, he was awarded Traditional Male Vocalist of the Year by the Society for the Preservation of Bluegrass Music of America (SPBGMA). In 1996, he became the first musician recognized by the South Carolina Bluegrass and Traditional Music Association and was presented the South Carolina Folk Heritage Award in 1998. For his good work in the community and business leadership, he was honored with the West Columbia Chamber of Commerce Lifetime Achievement Award. He received the Order of the Palmetto, the highest civilian honor in the state, awarded by the governor of South Carolina Nikki Haley. Bill Wells will long be revered as a champion of traditional-style bluegrass music in the Carolinas.

The Carolina Rebels. *Courtesy of Bill's Music Shop & Pickin' Parlor.*

Bill Wells and Rhonda Vincent. *Courtesy of Willie Wells.*

Opposite, bottom: Bill Wells (left) and Bluegrass icon Ralph Stanley (right). *Courtesy of Bill's Music Shop & Pickin' Parlor.*

Rhonda Vincent with Bill Wells on stage at Bill's Pickin' Parlor. *Courtesy of Bill's Music Shop and Pickin' Parlor & Willie Wells.*

WILLIE WELLS

After the passing of Bill Wells in 2011, his son, Willie Wells, stepped up to the helm of the Music Shop & Pickin' Parlor. Willie was committed to ensuring that the business and the music would continue. His mother, Louise, along with family members and devoted friends, is always there to help at the register, sell tickets and concessions, arrange seats and whatever else it takes. Willie Wells, an accomplished tenor singer and guitarist, was more than capable of keeping the Blue Ridge Mountain Grass band on stage and in high demand. The group performs in the tradition just as it did under the leadership of Bill. One of Bill's conditions for playing at the Parlor was his all-acoustic rule, which Willie Wells still maintains for bluegrass music. He said, "I have stuck to my guns on that for the bluegrass jam sessions, and that will never be compromised in honor of my dad and his wishes," he said. "The other nights, I have to diversify them just because of the type of music being presented."

If you have never been to Bill's Music Ship & Pickin' Parlor on a Friday, then you are missing something. Cars and trucks fill all the surrounding

Willie Wells. *Courtesy of Willie Wells.*

parking lots. Music is played on the stage, in the back rooms and in every corner of the music hall and store, even on the front porch. Willie Wells is doing much more than keeping the doors to a family business going. He is keeping the doors open to a home for bluegrass music in South Carolina. Willie explains it this way: "I'm absolutely dedicated to continuing what my dad has accomplished, promoting bluegrass and the bluegrass community."

5

Musicians & Champions, Traditions & Memories

B luegrass music is as much about the community as it is about the instruments. I hope these selected stories and memories reflect the bluegrass traditions and memories found in your own story.

MARTHA ADCOCK

We are all family on this earth, and despite the bad things we do to each other sometimes, we have to keep loving and keep trying to make things better for each other. My Christian faith sustains me, more so with every passing day.
—Martha Adcock

Martha grew up in Lee County near Bishopville, South Carolina. Both of her parents were musicians. Her mother worked in finance, and her father was a wonderful singer. Her father was so talented that Martha believes he could have been a professional big-band or pop singer, but with the onset of World War II, she said, her father came home to work on the large family farm. She said:

As the last available son to help his aging father, he raised his own family there as well. Farmers know about gambling! Nothing is under their control—not the weather, not the markets.

CAROLINA BLUEGRASS

Since I'd always been an artist and a dreamer interested in everything, they weren't too surprised at my determined choice, and probably from my childhood had been resigned to my fate [of becoming] an artist of some kind. I spent three years in college, but that was as long as I could be contained. For me, then, it was a choice between music and art, and I chose music. So my parents understood and accepted my willingness to take a chance with my music, and I believe they were proud that I was confident I could make a go of it. They accepted my choice with equanimity and encouragement.

Still, I remember the resigned look on their faces when they made one last stab and suggested I might think about a civil service career.

The only bluegrass music she heard as a child was on the local radio station, WAGS. The programming was actually a combination of country and rock 'n' roll music. As a teenager, Martha enjoyed playing and singing folk music. She said:

My interest in roots grew deeper, and I was drawn to old-timey style and then to bluegrass as some kind of genetic connection began to pull me in and cause me to travel to festivals in search of it. My "discovery" of bluegrass is, then, as much about finding it within myself as it is about learning a new skill. I had never known that both my grandfathers were fiddlers, as this information and the music was not passed directly to me by my parents early in my life. Our household's musical interests were opera, pop and classical, and I studied classical piano for eleven years. It was freeing to escape what I felt [were] the strict confines of these music styles and pursue uncharted, creative musical territory whose only traditions were unwritten ones.

By the time Martha was a young adult, the postwar bluegrass boom was starting to fade, as was heavy local touring by the likes of legends Flatt & Scruggs and Bill Monroe. However, radio and television shows out of Columbia and Charlotte featuring Pappy Sherrill, Snuffy Jenkins and Arthur Smith were still present. Martha would hunt through the record bins in search of her favorite big-label LPs of Ralph Stanley, Monroe, Flatt & Scruggs and the Stonemans. Like many of her peers, she also enjoyed pop music. She said, "Pat Boone gave way to the Beatles, and everything changed, except that R&B was a constant in our lives. We listened and danced to many different black groups on radio and records at home and in cars, live in auditoriums and clubs [and] at college and at the beach. To this day, my old classmates and I still love and can sing every word of all the R&B classics."

The 1960s proved to be an exciting time for Martha. She knew what she wanted to hear and where she needed to go to hear it.

When bluegrass festivals sprang up in the mid-'60s in Virginia and North Carolina, they became the holy grail that I pursued. After [I got a] taste of 'grass…at Union Grove, which…had been enough to raise the hair on the back of my neck, the all-bluegrass weekends put on by North Carolina promoter-songwriter Carlton Haney were heavenly, totally fulfilling. I saw and heard and experienced the Country Gentlemen, Dan Crary, Bill Monroe, Ralph Stanley, Lester Flatt, Mac Wiseman, Jimmy Martin, Don Reno, Bill Harrell and all the rest of the first generation of masters. I knew I'd found a home.

Pursuing a career in music has its ups and downs. This is something Martha has learned.

The road is definitely not an environment for everyone! It takes a special kind of person to be on the road. There are no routine days, even when you get home. You need to be extremely flexible in order to adapt to the vagaries of travel and playing and being your own boss, and your priorities often change from moment to moment, just like the many hats you must wear. Some people are completely unsuited for the road, those who have to have everything a certain way, their breakfast eggs exactly right, and all that. You have to go with the flow. The road is physically demanding for everyone, and there's no getting around that. We have it so much easier now than touring musicians did sixty years ago. I don't know how they survived the bad roads and the bad food and the general lack of amenities. The way they survived is the way we do today: you have to really have the desire to go pick and sing for folks.

If Martha could go back in time when she was just beginning her career, and even to the time when she was the little girl in Bishopville, she said:

I'd tell myself that nothing would ever be as easy again as it was right now, that life would be difficult at times, and that my ongoing battles would be mostly with myself. I'd tell myself just to keep the faith. But, of course, I wouldn't have had to tell myself any of that because I already knew it.

Left: Eddie & Marta Addock—June 1985, Nashville, Tennessee. *Photo taken by Martha with 35mm, timer and tripod.*

Below: Eddie & Martha Addock. *Courtesy of Bill's Music Shop & Pickin' Parlor.*

Thirty years ago, I held the opinion that thirty years from that point, the bluegrass umbrella would have grown: there would still be people playing traditional bluegrass, and there would also be people playing newgrass—our II Generation band's style of the day, which incorporated folk, blues, rock, jazz and more—and there would be people taking it even further out and away from bluegrass while still calling it bluegrass or some related "-grass" name. Those things have come to pass. Traditional bluegrass, even though Bill Monroe is gone, is still adhered to by many, although the younger generations aren't referencing tradition as often as they might. And as for the next thirty years, I foresee yet more barely imagined growth as well as a continued adherence to traditional forms by many faithful devotees.

Martha Adcock has many faithful devotees, and in the professional circle, she is described as a musician who plays a powerhouse style. The International Bluegrass Music Museum has designated her a "Pioneer." And according to *Bluegrass Now Magazine*: "Make no mistake—the clarity, passion and accuracy of Martha's leads easily place her among the top female singers in our business; maybe any business."

PAT AHRENS

Pat showed me a picture of herself as a child standing on a stage with another child; she was five years old and had been assigned to sing a solo in her church's Christmas pageant. Her mother had innocently given Pat her Christmas present early. It was a cowgirl toy cap pistol with a belt and holster. Arriving at the church, the choir director was dismayed to see that Pat had the holster and gun strapped around her waist. Shocking the adults, Pat announced that she would not sing without her gun! Fortunately, a compromise was reached when the director decided that the long, flowing white robe of Pat's angel costume would adequately cover her gun, and the show went on. At a very early age, Pat Ahrens has always danced to the beat of her own drum (or fiddle).

In Aiken, South Carolina, where Pat grew up, her father was a mechanic and volunteer firefighter. Her aunt played the organ, and Pat was attracted to music at a young age. In the early 1960s, Pat embraced the music and folk revival movement that was sweeping the country: "That was the most phenomenal era—look, I get chills just thinking about it, the fact that Baez,

Dylan, Ian and Sylvia, Lightfoot. I mean so many incredible musicians all came along at the same time. Those were the people…once you've ever heard that, your standards are just way on up there."

When it came to art, culture and music, Pat made it a habit to seek out the very best. When discussing commercialized music or the highly polished approach, she wrinkled her nose and said, "I'd rather hear the raw emotion of a real person." Pat had her first encounter with bluegrass music when she lived in Athens, Georgia.

I always hung out with all the artists. I've always gravitated toward the artists. A graduate student from Massachusetts had a party, everyone was playing and singing, and I sat in the corner and didn't say anything. All I knew was that I had never heard any music quite like it before. After he finished playing I asked him, "What do you call the music you just played?" He said, "Bluegrass." It was just like whoom; it hit me right between the eyes. It just did something to my heart.

Pat then moved from Athens to Columbia, South Carolina. Several of her musician friends familiar with the city told her, "There is a great banjo player there, and you've got to hear him. His name is Snuffy Jenkins." Not long after Pat moved, she found out that Jenkins worked at Central Chevrolet. She wanted to meet him and have him autograph her copy of *The New Lost City Ramblers Song Book*. So what did she do? "I baked him a cake and went down to Central Chevrolet and said, 'I want to hear you play. When are y'all playing next?" Jenkins took the cake and signed her book, and a new friendship began. That was in 1965. The autographed copy of the book was one of the first objects in her collection of bluegrass memorabilia. The book she has was also autographed by its coauthor John Cohen. Years later, when Cohen came to Columbia for his exhibit at the art museum, Pat was thrilled to get to meet him. She invited a group of musicians and Cohen to her home. She cooked dinner, and everyone played music for hours.

Pat continued to build her bluegrass friendships along with her collection. At one time, she owned every edition of *Bluegrass Unlimited* magazine. She has a copy of the November 1973 *Esquire* magazine, which featured an article called "The Return of the Banjo," also autographed by Snuffy Jenkins, who was mentioned by the author. Pat said, "I wouldn't take anything for it."

Pat has several filing cabinets dedicated to history, bands and musicians. One file she showed me featured the artwork of her friend North Carolina fiddle player and artist Jim Scancarelli. Jim is the cartoonist of *Gasoline Alley*.

Pat explained, "I have every one of the Christmas cards he's ever sent me. They feature the *Gasoline Alley* characters; he's wonderful!" She has other original items, including handwritten notes and letters from musicians and authors from all over the country. Pat is especially proud of her copy of a program from Bill Monroe's Grand Ole Opry Fiftieth Anniversary and a typed letter to Pat from Robert Shelton, a former folk music critic from the *New York Times*. Looking through the large book *The Face of Folk Music*, Pat said, "I get so doggone excited anytime anyone wants to look at this stuff. It just means so much to me." As a guitar player, singer, author, historian, folklorist and event producer, Pat has seen just about every bluegrass book and attended many festivals.

Pat attended the Galax, Virginia Fiddlers' Convention for more than twenty-one years, and she has been to Asheville First Class Bluegrass Fest and the Union Grove Fiddlers Convention for more than twelve years. She has served as a band contest judge at Reno Fest in Hartsville, South Carolina, and as emcee for the Congaree Bluegrass Festival in Cayce, South Carolina, and you will always find Pat serving as the emcee of Friday night's open stage at Bill's Music Shop. Her longtime friend Ashley Carder said:

> *I can't remember exactly when I met Pat. My first memories of her are from a jam session that used to be held at a community center near Ballentine in the early 1980s. It seems like you'd see Pat any place where there was bluegrass music or banjos and fiddles. Pat has been a good friend of mine since the 1980s. She is a big fan of fiddle tunes and always loved to play the guitar while I was playing old fiddle tunes. Pat is a wonderful lady and is a fine singer and guitar player. She has done a lot for the music and has done a great service to the music community by documenting the music and writing articles and books about our regional musicians. She wrote the book on Snuffy Jenkins and Pappy Sherrill and also wrote books on Bill Wells [and] Tut Taylor and helped Butch Robins with his book. Pat also wrote a book in the early 1970s on the Union Grove Fiddlers Convention. Pat continues to be a champion for the music, and you can find her at Bill's Music Shop nearly every Friday night, where she emcees the open stage. Some of my favorite times with Pat are the times we played together on stage at the Galax Old Time Fiddle Convention. I would definitely call her the First Lady of South Carolina bluegrass music.*

Today, Pat is a freelance writer. She is the author of *Union Grove: The First Fifty Years*, *The Legacy of Two Legends* and *Bill Wells Bluegrass Ambassador*. Pat has coauthored banjoist Butch Robins's book, *What I Know 'Bout What I Know*.

Books authored and coauthored by Pat Ahrens. *Courtesy of Pat Ahrens.*

A 1987 personal license plate. (The first bluegrass license plate in the state of South Carolina was issued to Pat). *Courtesy of Pat Ahrens.*

This book was nominated by the International Bluegrass Music Association as Print Media Personality of the Year for 2004. She has coauthored with Tut Taylor *Tut Taylor: The Flat Pickin' Dobro® Man* and is the biographer of banjoist "Snuffy" Jenkins. Pat is co-founder of the South Carolina Bluegrass and Traditional Music Association and a past president. She served on the association's board of directors from 1991 to 2006. She has had numerous articles printed through the years, some of which have appeared in the magazine *Bluegrass Unlimited*. In addition, she has written liner notes for several CDs.

In 1992, Pat served on a committee involved with a unique music event for the South Carolina State Museum. The event had a country music theme that included live performances. Pat designed an exhibit on bluegrass music history from her personal, extensive private collection. In 1996, Pat was honored with the Jean Laney Harris South Carolina Folk Heritage Music Advocacy Award. The song she chose to sing for the event was written by James Randolph and entitled "In Old Carolina." The caption beneath her photograph in her college yearbook seems to have said it all: "Patricia Louise Johnson, She shall have music wherever she goes."

AIKEN BLUEGRASS FESTIVAL

With all the outstanding bluegrass bands and people who want to hear the music live, the Carolinas can never have too many outstanding bluegrass festivals.

When she thinks about how the Aiken Bluegrass Festival started, Molly Groat Schaumann said, "Twelve years ago, my dad had a crazy idea. He loved music, but he didn't have any musical talent." What Steve Groat did have was a commitment and love for the STAR riding program, a therapeutic riding organization, and for the town of Aiken. He wanted to find a way to combine his love for both. Steve created a festival that would bring top-quality music to Aiken and help raise funds for the deserving nonprofit. According to Molly, "He slowly recruited my mother and sister and I to help out. By the second or third year, I recruited [my husband] Christian." When Steve passed away in 2014, Christian was willing and able to take over the reins. By 2015, the festival attracted almost ten thousand people.

The festival has had many bluegrass champions, including community members, volunteers and, most importantly, the bands and musicians themselves. Some of the early bands were Sam Bush, Dixie Beeliners, Steep Canyon Rangers, Peter Rowan & Tony Rice, Mountain Heart, Acoustic Syndicate, Old Crow Medicine Show, John Cowan, Della Mae, Infamous Stringdusters, Iron Horse and Hackensack Boys. Recent bands to attend are Greensky Bluegrass, Larry Keel, Jeremy Garrett, Andy Hall, Jon Stickley, Dave Bruzza, Paul Hoffman, Town Mountain, Keller Williams, Keller and the Keels, the Travelin' McCourys and Doug and the Henrys. Special individuals, such as Larry Keel, have been with Christian and Molly for so many years he is part of the festival family.

It was not always easy. In the beginning, people would give the family a confused look and say, "I don't like country music." Molly and Christian realized that people wound need to hear and experience bluegrass firsthand. The family also had to learn a few things. The first year, the headliner band pulled up in the bus, and although the festival tent was ready, there was nothing for the musicians to sit on, no place to relax. The band had to bring furniture out of its bus to create a "green room." The event grew so fast that area hotels could not accommodate the tourists. Christian and Molly changed the event from being a downtown street fair to a full-fledged bluegrass destination with vendors, hospitality for bands and camping. The magic was in the music. Molly said there were no divas: "The bands knew and liked one another. They were friends. We got lucky because that's where the magic is at."

Christian continues to take his leadership role and responsibilities seriously. He works with the town, books the talent, secures permits and sponsors and keeps up with all the financial demands of a large-scale public event. Molly recalls prior to her father's illness, he would stand on stage and look at the crowd of people all coming together for bluegrass in Aiken. She could see how proud he was. In fact, sometimes during the festival, she can still envision him standing on the side of the stage, arms folded, smiling and listening to the music.

Much has changed. People no longer look confused when you say "bluegrass," and you have to believe that Steve would be prouder than ever. He would be proud of his town, his family and his festival. Because of the music, STAR riding continues to thrive. People look forward to having another family-friendly festival where they can hear bluegrass music performed live, just the way it was meant to be. Perhaps that is the reason why the magic in Aiken continues to happen.

For more information about the Aiken Bluegrass Festival, visit Aikenbluegrassfestival.org or check them out on Facebook.

ROGER BELLOW

Roger grew up in Chicago; his mother was a social worker at a community settlement house. By the early twentieth century, urban communities experienced a wide variety of social issues due to the problems associated with industrial life. Settlement houses provided services for families seeking work and better living conditions. Some of these families were immigrants; many of them were from the southern Appalachian Mountain region. Healthcare, food programs, daycare and vocational schools were some of the programs offered to the poor white southerners who had come north to work in the factories.

As a child, Roger would visit the settlement house; he made friends, and he learned a great deal about southern culture, arts, crafts, storytelling and traditional mountain music. During the 1960s bluegrass revival and folk festivals, Roger was exposed to the artists who took part in the large events hosted at the university. In many ways, he believes he had the best of both worlds. When Roger's mother was ready to move away from Chicago's cold weather for a warmer climate, she spontaneously chose South Carolina. By that time, Roger was already a passionate, skilled musician and traveler.

Roger received his bachelor's degree in Spanish from the University of Tennessee and studied at the Universidad Nacional de México and the Centro de Estudios Colombo-Americanos in Bogotá, Colombia. He taught conversational Spanish at the Sullivan Language School in Chicago. By the time the family arrived on Sullivan's Island, he was ready to start a career in radio. It had been difficult to break into the radio business in the Windy City, but the smaller South Carolina market was more receptive.

Roger's persistence paid off. The station manager at WSCI-FM 89.3 agreed and seemed interested and willing to give Roger a chance, so he started right away. A few months after he began, his benefactor was dismissed from the station, but since Roger was already on the air, they let him stay. This was the beginning of some of what Roger calls the best years of his professional life. For fifteen years, Roger hosted Vintage Country on WSCI public radio in Charleston. Through most of the 1990s, the *Yorktown* battleship housed WSCI-FM 89.3, a local public radio station, which was part of the South Carolina Educational Radio Network. WSCI's offices and library were inside while its broadcast booth was in the ship's "pri-fly" (primary flight control), which is the control tower of the aircraft carrier overlooking the water, facing the Charleston peninsula. Roger said he still remembers how he would have to carry a heavy box of vinyl records up the long narrow flight of stairs. This is also where he met Gary Erwin, "Shrimp City Slim." Gary said:

> *Our radio programs (his* Vintage Country *and my* Blues in the Night*) were on back-to-back hours for a while on WSCI 89.3 FM. I always*

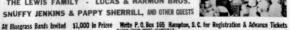

Above: Roger Bellow and the Drifting Troubadours. *Courtesy of Bill's Music Shop & Pickin' Parlor.*

Left: Vintage 1971 Low Country Bluegrass Festival poster. *Courtesy of Ashley Carder.*

thought it was an interesting segue because of the historic relationship between blues and country music. Many members of both musical communities grew up listening to and learning from the other. Those big radio stations in the 1940s and 1950s broadcast both styles resoundingly through the South, with huge audiences of both black and white. Plus, as many have recognized, both styles really preserve the story-in-song approach, which is so important. Roger released several albums on Flying Fish Records (the label owned by Bruce Kaplan in Chicago and distributed by Rounder). He also played on two of my albums: Blues on the Beach *(1994) and* Blue Palmetto *(1996). Roger and I also were the Bayou Ramblers in the Cajun band Paul Kershaw & the Bayou Ramblers. Mr. Kershaw who was in his seventies at the time (from Kaplan, Louisiana, oddly enough). We traveled the Southeast playing traditional Cajun music (Roger, fiddle, guitar and bass; I played washboard and drums). We cut one CD,* Allons a Grand Kaplan, *on Erwin Music (my label) in 1998.*

Roger and Gary have maintained their friendship to this day. Roger shared the stage with many artists, including Paul Anistasio, Johnny Gimble, Liz Masterson and Sean Blackburn. He worked for the South Carolina Arts Commission and was hired to teach and perform in schools throughout the state. He has performed acoustic country, swing and bluegrass music in Charleston for over twenty years while performing all over the world.

In 1995, Roger received the South Carolina Jean Laney Harris Folk Heritage Award. Roger continues to perform; leads his Texas-style western swing group, the Drifting Troubadours; and teaches Spanish to local students through classic Mexican folk songs. It only makes sense that *Bluegrass Unlimited* called him "a member of the elite circle of superlative pickers."

ALAN BIBEY

Alan is said to be one of the most creative and technically gifted mandolinists in bluegrass and acoustic music. He grew up in Walnut Cove, North Carolina, and started playing when he was five years old. His father, James Bibey, played mandolin. Alan said:

My dad took me to see Bill Monroe when I was five, and I came home and just always knew from that moment on that, that was what I wanted to do.

My dad told me when I got better than him he was gonna switch to banjo, which is funny because he had never played banjo but he was just a really good musician. So one day, when I'm like seven, he switches to playing banjo and never plays mandolin again.

Alan recalls there were fiddler conventions almost every weekend in North Carolina. His father took him to compete at the Madison-Mayodan Bluegrass Festival, his first competition, and he won the third-place prize of five dollars. He said, "I was hooked after that." The mandolin was his first instrument; he picked up guitar, fiddle, banjo and bass along the way. As a teenager, he played throughout North and South Carolina. James Bibey continued to teach his son and mentored other young musicians as well. Alan said:

My dad taught me everything I know, and he also taught my first cousin Gary Brown, who has been playing at the Carolina Opry in Myrtle Beach for the last twenty-five years and [is] another super musician. Gary was four years older than me and had been out playing professionally some and gave me some great technique tips on how and what I should be practicing. That's the closest thing I ever had to a formal lesson.

Things progressed quickly. By the time he was sixteen, he was playing all over North and South Carolina. Shortly, he won first place at the World's Fair in Knoxville and received an invitation to join the groundbreaking band the New Quicksilver and worked as one of the original members. Alan has worked with IIIrd Tyme Out and BlueRidge. In the late '90s, Alan worked with groups such as Baucom, Bibey & Blueridge and Baucom, Bibey, Graham & Haley.

He won the IBMA "Instrumental Album of the Year" in 2001, the 2004 BlueRidge project for which he wrote the title track and was nominated for a Grammy. He was included in the Mel Bay book *Greatest Mandolin Players of the Twentieth Century*. He won the Society for the Preservation of Bluegrass Music of America (SPBGMA) Mandolin Performer of the Year in 2007, 2009 and 2010 and the SPBGMA Album of the Year in 2006 and 2008. He has had numerous No. 1 albums and songs, including Grasstowne's 2014 *Cold Dark Ground*, on which he collaborated with Mark Collie and Ronnie Bowman. *The Mandolin Chronicles* (2012) was nominated last year for five IBMA awards. In early 2004, the Gibson Company put into production the Alan Bibey Signature line of mandolins, reaffirming his status as one of the most influential mandolin players in bluegrass and acoustic music history. Currently Alan plays with his band Grasstowne and is working on several albums for various artists that he produces in his studio, Maggie's Crib, in Surfside Beach, South Carolina.

CURTIS BLACKWELL

Curtis Blackwell was eight years old when his eldest brother, V.V. Blackwell, allowed him to play his guitar. V.V. drew lines for the frets and put dots where his little brother should place his fingers and Curtis taught himself to play. Two years later, Curtis made his debut performance at church.

In the '50s and '60s, Curtis played both the banjo and guitar and was writing his own songs. In 1960, Curtis and two friends won a radio talent contest. The grand prize included an opportunity for Curtis, his brother Haskell and their friend Junior Crowe to perform at the Grand Ole Opry. The station manager Gene Bolinger drove the young men to Nashville. It was an exciting moment, and as Curtis said, "The radio station bought us brand new suits, all black. We looked and felt like Johnny Cash." In 1965, the three men formed the Dixie Bluegrass Boys. Curtis played guitar, Al Osteen played banjo, Larry Jefferson played mandolin, Sam Cobb played bass and Randall Collins played fiddle. The group toured throughout the East Coast for more than ten years. In 1970, they won the contest for bands at the Union Grove Fiddlers Convention. The group went on to win first place at the Union Grove Bluegrass Festival.

The Dixie Bluegrass Boys have played for many stars that include North Carolina icons the William Brothers, Loretta Lynn, Carl Smith, Conway Twitty and others. The band has also opened for the Dale McCoury and Boys.

Curtis has much to be proud of, from traveling on the road and playing with Bill Monroe in 1967 to an incredibly long and fulfilling career with the Dixie Bluegrass Boys for over fifty years. The North Carolina–based band consists of founding members, Curtis Blackwell and Sam Cobb, joined by banjo player Charles Wood, fiddler Chuck Nations and mandolinist Vic Backwell. Curtis has been honored in the Atlanta Music Hall of Fame, and in 2012, the Dixie Bluegrass Boys performed a twelve-show tour in Ireland. However, one of his greatest joys, as he explained, is playing with a group that has allowed him to "be part of a band that has included some of the best musicians you could ever dream of being part of."

CHRIS BOUTWELL

Chris Boutwell, originally from California, has played traditional bluegrass music since the 1960s. He taught himself by spending time with experienced musicians. Chris's professional career started when he was in his twenties, as a guitarist with the California-based High Country. The music scene on the West Coast was flourishing with the folk revivals. Chris recorded several albums on the Warner Brothers label and performed with early bluegrass veterans Vern Williams and Ray Park, the first musicians to have a traditional bluegrass band in California.

In 1982, Chris and his family moved to South Carolina, and he wasted no time getting involved with the bluegrass community. Chris has played with

High Country record cover, Chris Boutwell center. *Courtesy of Ashley Carder.*

a variety of groups, including the Palmetto String Band, Amick Junction, the Claude Lucas Band, High Lonesome, Anna and Shellie Davis and the Unnamed Bluegrass Band. Chris currently plays with, and is a founding member of, Palmetto Blue and takes a special interest in coaching young musicians. When you attend a Palmetto Blue concert, you will not only hear great music but also learn a thing or two, as Chris shares facts about the history of the music, as well as tells humorous and interesting stories about the origins of the songs. Fellow band member Ashley Carder said, "To those who know him, he is considered a 'walking encyclopedia' of bluegrass knowledge and is eager to share with those around him."

Chris is a singer and a yodeler, master of the mandolin, rhythm guitar and banjo player who enjoys playing banjo in the three-finger style popularized by Earl Scruggs in the 1940s. Chris plays regularly with Palmetto Blue at venues throughout the Midlands, including the Columbia Museum of Art, the University of South Carolina and Bill's Pickin' Parlor. Chris Boutwell is a member of the Lone Star Bluegrass and Country Music Hall of Fame. Chris was awarded South Carolina's Jean Laney Harris Folk Heritage award in 2014 for his dedication to preserving traditional bluegrass music.

ASHLEY CARDER

Ashley is committed to sharing everything he knows about bluegrass and old-time music with the next generation of pickers. He is witty, soft spoken and intelligent. When it comes to fiddling, Ashley has already forgotten more than most folks ever knew.

Shirley, his mother, played music and sang on the South Carolina WBLR Batesburg/Leesville radio station's live broadcast, *Ridge Jamboree*, during the late '60s. Mrs. Carder sang with a country band, the Swinging Countrymen, and other groups. Ashley said, "I would listen to her play on the radio broadcast and at home. I taught myself to play guitar around 1969." Around 1980, Carder was in the Easley, South Carolina area and had taken a break from college. He was working with his father on construction jobs while he tried to figure out what he wanted to do. Some of the men on the work crew would sit around during their lunch break and play the banjo and guitar, and he became interested in playing the banjo. He remembers going to a pawnshop in Spartanburg, where, he said, "I found a banjo and bought it for seventy-five dollars." Ashley learned several things during this time. He learned he didn't want to keep working construction and that he really liked bluegrass music. He also learned that compared to construction work, college wasn't all that bad, so he returned to Wofford College and finished his degree.

During his college years, he started attending nearby bluegrass festivals, and at events like the Little Mountain Festival, he met aspiring and accomplished musicians who lived near his hometown of Leesville. He met guitarist Carlin Padgett, who had actually performed with Ashley's mother, Shirley, during the radio days, and Ashley Carder took it all in. By the time Carder was in his early twenties, he said, "My dad gave me his grandfather Carder's old fiddle, and I really took an interest in playing the fiddle. I learned fiddle by hanging out with the old guys during the early 1980s." Young men learning to fiddle from old men who had learned to fiddle from other old men, that's traditionally how bluegrass is taught. Carder said, "I learned from Vernon Riddle [1935–2011] of Spartanburg, Bo Norris [1910–1987] of Ward and Pappy Sherrill [1915–2001] of Chapin." Carder would see Pappy at the festivals and was often invited to the Sherrill home to visit, listen and play music. Ashley made a habit of bringing his tape recorder along. He recalled, "On those visits I would sit and play guitar, and Pappy would play the fiddle. When I went home I would get my fiddle, use my tape player and sit and mess with the fiddle to learn Pappy's licks." Associating with the senior men, Ashley heard some of the more obscure old-time music that old-timers, such as Saluda County's Bo Norris, liked to play. He said that "Skid Row" and "Down in Georgia on a Hog" were the kinds of songs Bo Norris had learned from two old men back in the 1920s. Bo explained that he had learned these songs from "Old man Gregory and Old Man Ed-erds, both of whom lived near Bo when he was young." Ashley explained that the name was actually Edwards, but Bo Norris would always pronounce it "Ed-erds."

Ashley became close friends with these men regardless of the age difference; they shared a deep love for the bluegrass and old-time fiddle. When many of the men passed away, their family members reached out to Ashley to see if he might like items from their personal effects. Certainly the instruments and career mementos should be passed on to someone who would honor the legacy. Ashley Carder is exactly that kind of "someone." Today, Ashley Carder has an impressive collection of photographs and memorabilia, which serve as a constant reminder of his dear friends and mentors. This includes a room full of fiddles, over one hundred to be exact.

I first met Wade Eugene "W.E." Leitner around 1980 when I was just getting involved in bluegrass and old-time music. He was a house builder by

Above: W.E. Leitner, rehairing a fiddle bow. Lexington, South Carolina. *Courtesy of Ashley Carder.*

Right: George Pritchard of North Augusta, South Carolina, wrote this letter to fiddle maker W.E. Leitner in 1982. *Courtesy of Ashley Carder.*

May 12, 1982

Dear Mr. Leitner,

I received my Bows today. Let me say to you they look great. You do a very good job and I am going to bring you some more to Rehair. (Just don't raise the price now that I think you are good. Ha ha!)

I will tell friends I meet at the Festivals you do good work, Maybe they will contact you. I won't mention price but will tell them you do quality work at low prices.

You didn't charge me for the Frog so I am going to make a check out for $45.00 instead of $39.00.

Again thanks you for doing a good job on my Bows.

Sincerely,
George Pritchard

trade, but made and repaired fiddles in a small shop attached to his carport at his home between Lexington and West Columbia. He later built a larger shop in his backyard over the top of an in-ground swimming pool that he no longer used. Mr. Leitner told me that he started making instruments after he and his bluegrass-playing son-in-law were having a discussion one day, and the son-in-law said that he was a good cabinetmaker and carpenter but that he bet he couldn't make a fiddle. Mr. Leitner then found some plans on how to build a violin, and he made one. He proceeded to make over sixty fiddles from the late 1970s until his death in 2010. Mr. Leitner also made guitars and an occasional mandolin, banjo or Dobro[®]*. He was totally self-taught and would often experiment with different designs, such as a fiddle with the sound holes on the side instead of the top. His instruments often had quite a good sound, and most of the fiddlers in the area during the 1980 to 2010 time frame owned a Leitner fiddle. Among the fiddlers who played Leitner instruments were Homer "Pappy" Sherrill, Don Ashley, Olin Sizemore and myself. I have even run across a fiddler at a fiddlers convention in Virginia whose favorite instrument was his Leitner fiddle. From around 1980 until his death, Mr. Leitner was a fixture at bluegrass festivals and fiddlers conventions throughout the southeastern United States, where he would set up his camper and tables and sell instruments, strings, picks and other accessories and would rehair fiddle bows all day long. At the festivals, Mr. Leitner was easily recognizable with his old-fashioned bib overalls and his tables full of fiddles lined up in a row. Mr. Leitner received South Carolina's Jean Laney Harris Folk Heritage Award in 1996 for instrument making. He built my home in 2001 when he was seventy-five years old. After his death, I acquired most of his luthier tools, instruments and accessories, and I have been busy restoring many dusty old fiddles from his shop.*

When Spartanburg, South Carolina native Vernon Riddle passed away in 2011, his wife, Ruth, gave her late husband's fiddle to Ashley Carder. Ashley wrote a summary describing Mr. Riddle's contributions and awards. The paragraph appeared in the *Old-Time Herald* magazine. It read as follows:

Vernon Riddle, was born in 1935, in Glendale, South Carolina[, and] was known to the traditional music community as a fine Texas-style old-time fiddler. While he was serving in the US Air Force and stationed in Texas from 1955 to 1975, he developed and refined his fiddling style by spending lots of time with Eck Robertson, Jack Mears, Benny Thomasson, Texas Shorty, Vernon and Norman Solomon and others. Vernon played many of Eck

Robertson's old tunes that might otherwise have been forgotten. Vernon was a quiet, soft-spoken person, but he was always willing to share his music with others. In 2010 the Field Recorders' Collective released a CD of his fiddling from the 1960s through the early 1990s. In addition to placing in many Texas fiddle contests in the 1960s and '70s, Vernon won the South Carolina State Fiddling Competition Championship, and the Lunsford Award for Significant Contributions to Music in 2007, and he was a recipient of the Jean Laney Harris Folk Heritage Award from the State of South Carolina in 1999.

In 2012, Ashley Carder received the Jean Laney Harris Folk Heritage Award Traditional Fiddling and preservation of South Carolina's fiddle traditions.

SHELLIE DAVIS

Shellie picked up her first instrument at eight years old. Her sister had just started with banjo lessons, and as the younger sibling, she didn't want to be left out. So Shellie chose to learn to play the bass. Shellie said, "As you can probably guess, as an eight-year-old, bluegrass was not my first choice when it came to the kind of music I wanted to play. At that point I knew nothing about it and simply labeled it as 'old people music.' I now know that I was completely wrong."

It wasn't long before Shellie found her way to Bill's Pickin' Parlor. She said, "The first time I went to Bill's, I was probably around nine or ten years old. I remember being surprised by how many people could fit into this one small building and amazed by the amount of people who were completely in love and devoted to bluegrass music.

Shellie believes that bluegrass music is unique in its history and that it combines instruments together like no other genre. She has found the community to be a close-knit, diverse group of people. "The music brings together people of all ages from all different backgrounds," she said. As a child she enjoyed the fall festival held in her hometown, Batesburg-Leesville. During one of these early events where she was playing, she remembers, "I was nine years old, and at the time, I had just started losing my voice. Halfway through a song my voice cracked, my sister laughed and I cried and ran off stage as fast as I could!"

Shellie has come a long way since those days, and no one would ever guess that the self-assured young woman performing with Palmetto Blue had ever felt uncomfortable on the stage. Certainly, the band has been a great experience for her, as she admits:

Yes, being the youngest in a band of men over fifty may not seem like the most exciting thing for a seventeen-year-old girl, but I wouldn't have it any other way. Their experience and faith in me have pushed me to be a better musician and all-around better person. Though the time we have left together is uncertain, I am thankful for the impact that these people and their love for music has made on my life.

CLARENCE DREHER, PRODUCER OF *THE BLUEGRASS SOUND*

The Bluegrass Sound started in July 1983 on South Carolina Educational Radio. The program has always included a variety of traditional and contemporary bluegrass music along with well-loved old-time mountain music. This popular show has never been a "drop the needle" type of program. Thanks to the show's creator, Clarence Dreher, listeners have come to count on hearing the right combination of live recorded music, interviews with well-known bluegrass performers, regional favorites and concerts by top-notch talent. Clarence has been the producer since the show began in 1983.

Clarence recalls a trip the family made when he was about twelve years old. His father, who was also Columbia's mayor at the time, attended the International Lions Club Convention in Chicago. At the convention, the South Carolina Lions Chapter was giving away small brooms to support the Lions charity efforts for the blind. The convention hall was full of people from all over the world. His father had arranged for Snuffy Jenkins and Pappy Sherrill also to perform at the event. As the South Carolina Lions distributed the brooms, the men played music, and everyone crowded near to listen. The effect the music had on the audience is something that Clarence never forgot.

It appears that bluegrass music and Clarence have somehow managed to always cross paths. Clarence and his wife, Donna, are longtime members and supporters of SCETV and radio. He appreciated the programming and began listening to a bluegrass show that aired for thirty minutes on Saturday morning at 6:00 a.m. If you missed the Saturday broadcast you could hear it again on Wednesday afternoons at 2:00 p.m. Clarence believes the best way to listen to bluegrass is to hear it live; however, at that time, radio was the next-best thing.

When the show ended in 1982, like many people, Clarence was very disappointed. Clarence contacted the executive director of South Carolina Educational Radio to make a suggestion, he said: "I got in touch with Bill

Hay, who was in charge of SCERN, and told him they should find a way to keep the program on the air or start another program. Bill said, 'We would be glad to. Why don't you do it?'"

Clarence took on the challenge for a three-month trial period. He was the producer, and Patti Just was the first program host. The new program caught on, and three months has become thirty-two years. After Patti moved to the ETV station in Sumter, Dr. Gary Stanton became the second host. Gary moved out of state, and when Clarence met Columbia newcomer and bluegrass enthusiast Dr. Larry Klein, he knew that this was the man for the job. The partnership between Clarence and Larry has been great, and for the past twenty-seven years, Larry Klein been hosting the program with Clarence as producer.

The radio industry has changed since those early days when they were located on Millwood Avenue. Clarence remembers the interviews with greats like Bill Monroe and Earl Scruggs. The first festival he ever attended was the Snuffy Jenkins Festival, and he conducted six to eight interviews at that event. He interviewed Ralph Stanley, who spoke about the days when they would put four or five men to ride all day and all night in a car with a bass fiddle tied on top. Being on the road traveling from one gig to the next was exhausting in the early days. Clarence interviewed one now well-known performer while they were playing at a club in the Five Points neighborhood of Columbia. The club was very small with no quiet place to conduct the interview. Clarence and the team escorted the band member to the only quiet place they could find—a single stall bathroom. They put down the commode seat down and made their guest as comfortable as possible. Things have indeed changed a great deal.

An active member of the IBMA, Clarence is proud of the contributions the Carolinas have made to the genre. He said:

> *The three-finger style of the five-string banjo, that was developed by Snuffy Jenkins, of course. Earl Scruggs took it and refined it. The Carolinas banjo style put a lot of drive in to the music. If you take a compass and draw a circle around Northwest South Carolina and Southwest North Carolina, you've got the birthplace of Snuffy Jenkins, Earl Scruggs and Don Reno, that was just the place that the three-finger style originated and was perfected.*

North Carolina fiddle player Bobby Hicks, who played with Ricky Skaggs and Kentucky Thunder, and Balsam Range banjoist Marc Pruett are a few of Clarence's personal favorites. Marc was one of the first people he ever interviewed. Marc Pruett played at the Fiddling Pig in Asheville, and the musicians he played with became the members of Balsam Range. "They have incredible instrumentation and great vocal harmonies" Clarence said.

Another talented band is Steep Canyon Rangers. Clarence explained, "The story goes that Steve Martin's wife is from North Carolina, and about eight to ten years ago, they were here visiting with her family. They were at a party where Steep Canyon Rangers was playing. Steve picked up his banjo and started to play with them. Now, that's the band he likes to use when travels and plays."

Producing the radio show has been a labor of love, very rewarding and a great deal of fun. Today, Clarence helps his son, Jay, in a business they purchased five years ago, PlayBetterBluegrass.com. The company is an e-commerce business committed to providing the very best musical instruments, musical accessories, instructional books and DVDs covering various how-to topics.

After all these years, Clarence and bluegrass not only crossed paths but also continued on a parallel journey. And this is a road he cheerfully travels today. He said, "I stumbled onto it. I enjoyed the music, and well, I just really cared about it."

The Bluegrass Sound can be heard on each Saturday from 9:00 to 10:00 p.m. on South Carolina Public Radio.

JIM GRADDICK

Jim was born in Columbia and raised in Blythewood. His grandfather plays the guitar, and in the 1800s, his great-great-grandfather was a violinist with the Columbia Symphony. The sound of fiddle is special to him. Jim describes it by saying, "I suppose the fiddle is more like a bird than anything else. Songs like "Cluck Old Hen," "Chicken Reel" and "Listen to the Mockingbird" are all standard tunes for a fiddle player. Fiddlers are the soprano voices of the bluegrass band so it's only natural that we get compared to birds squawking or chirping."

Following along the classical music path, as a middle school student, Jim played the violin in the Blythewood Middle School Orchestra. He was already interested in bluegrass music. However, as he stated, he chose the violin, "because they [the school orchestra] didn't offer banjo!"

Jim always loved music but did not get serious about playing until he realized he could make people happy and make money at the same time. So the young man pushed himself in the school orchestra and also joined the Strolling Strings. Being in the group was a way to fundraise for field trips and paid five dollars a night. If you know Jim Graddick, then you know he loves to perform and is very competitive. He eventually became concertmaster in the local school district. His skill, energy and drive had him sitting in with bands at age fifteen. Jim was gigging in restaurants for tip money and found a home away from home playing at Bill's Pickin' Parlor. The time he spent at Bill's provided the bulk of his nonclassical education.

With their welcoming personalities, bluegrass musicians brought the young musician into the family fold. Jim recalls:

> When I started I didn't know anyone, but all the musicians welcomed me into their circles and taught me their songs and traditions. They seemed to have infinite patience when I struggled and infinite joy when I played the songs correctly. Dr. Ralph Cox, Danny Harlow and Jason Kelly were my first teachers in the bluegrass world and they never wanted a dime for all of their hard work.

To play the fiddle as well as Jim, it takes work and apparently some suffering. Jim said:

> I have played until my jaw bleeds and my collarbone stays bruised. Every upper string player develops a spot under the chin similar to a callus. It's a source of pride along with our hardened fingertip calluses (touch screens are hard to use, and we have no fingerprints left on our left hands). The goal is to entertain, but I try to add new things to each performance since I never have time to practice. I guess my ultimate goal is to have complete control over my instrument, but I'm sure that will never happen. Even Jascha Heifetz struggled with his limitations. It's those struggles that help me relate to my students in their musical journey.

A large part of Jim's journey includes Bill's Pickn' Parlor. "The stage at Bill's is my second home. I have spent more time on that stage than anyone else. I feel totally at home there," he said.

Jim stays on the road and appears to take his fiddle everywhere he goes. He has opinions about everything from fast food to politics and expresses them with his tongue-in-cheek sense of humor. Although he spends so much time entertaining and with his musician friends, Jim's not exactly what one would call an extrovert. One of his favorite places to play music is actually in the studio. He said, "I love playing in a studio because it is the quietest place I've ever been. Sometimes the absence of music will force your mind to become more independent musically. You aren't trying to re-create anything but what is in your mind."

You might think that Jim's classical training and dedication to perfecting his craft would make him some sort of bluegrass snob (if there is such a thing); that is not the case at all. According to Jim, "It's the imperfections that provide the allure. It makes people think, 'Maybe I could do that!' You don't have to be a celebrity to do it or be the greatest musician in the world. It's totally focused on joy. The joy of the audience and the performer is paramount. No record deals or corporate fat-cats needed!"

Jim Graddick is a talented young South Carolina fiddle player with plenty of joy.

HASTINGS HENSEL

Hastings Hensel is an author and poet. His creative nonfiction has been published in *South Carolina Living, Coastal Isles, Grand Strand* and *Coastal Carolina Life*. Recent articles on bluegrass, the great bluegrass roadshow and Carolina bluegrass all-stars (2014) are excellent resources on the local bluegrass scene. Hastings said:

> *I believe that picking parlors in South Carolina are undoubtedly special places. I love how democratic the process is: everyone and anyone can play, and the songs are the currency, the common language. Democracy and bluegrass are all about the fluid relationship between the group and the individual, but part of that involves a meritocratic system in which the best pickers have their "voice" heard more often, something like elected officials. After all, the solo is ideally supposed to mimic the melody of the voice, what has just been sung.*
>
> *Obviously, solos give a great picker the chance to show off his or her skills, but I also noticed that the best pickers approached solos almost like jazz musicians, as ways to give new life to old songs through imaginative riffs.*
>
> *And so bluegrass, in my opinion, reflects the best of our country's democracy in that conservatism and progressiveness are in dialogue with one another. People in these parlors play the same songs, and will be doing so in twenty years, but new generations of talent are also infusing bluegrass with other musical*

styles—hence such hybrid genres as punk-grass, brew-grass, gangstagrass, etc. I think the first country/gospel/bluegrass band I ever heard—and it sort of behooves me to admit this—was the Oak Ridge Mountain Boys singing "Elvira" as I danced the two-step at junior cotillion in Columbia, South Carolina, when I was twelve or thirteen years old. There was something very different about that song, something I'd never head before—the haunting high lonesome voice and a boom-chuck rhythm.

In the twenty years since, I have been to many bluegrass festivals and bluegrass concerts, but it wasn't until I visited the South Carolina picking parlors as a freelance writer that I understood how communal the genre's roots are. I'll never forget my interview with Keisler Tanner at Homespun in Chesnee. He was so eloquent and passionate and thankful that I had—and this is no embellishment—tears in my eyes as he talked about what bluegrass means to his community. And he pointed out that many players make their way from the picking parlor to the local stage and then to the national festivals—the American dream of upward mobility right there, but in bluegrass music.

ROGER HOWELL

Roger Howell has always lived in Madison County. His grandmother Sina Thomas Howell occasionally played the guitar and piano, one of the only people in his early family who could play music. Roger said:

My grandpa got a little old RCA wind-up Victrola from a local department store. It came with a few 78 rpm records of the day, including [those of] the Carter Family, Bradley Kincade and Ernest V. Stoneman. My dad, Orville V. Howell, a self-educated radio and TV repairman, built one of the first television sets in town [in 1952]. My dad and mom always kept records and listened to lots of music in the home, too, from a wide variety of singers, country-western, pop, swing, you name it. I grew up in a very musically diverse setting, with many recorded artists at my disposal. Although nobody in the family played a musical instrument, I was always surrounded by music. My mother kept the record player and radio going when I was small, and her favorites were Marty Robbins, Pat Boone, Chet Atkins, Jerry Lee Lewis, Johnny Cash, Fats Domino, Perry Como, Jimmy Rogers and Glen Miller. My musical tastes were very wide and formed from this early and mid-1950s music, and I still love it and listen to it often today. But my favorite is still the very early country music, with old mountain music (often referred to as "hillbilly") being a close second, believe it or not. A lot of people are surprised at that, since I'm known mostly for playing the fiddle. But I'm a lover of old country music, first and foremost. My favorite time of the week growing up in the early 1960s was Saturday afternoons, when the old black-and-white country music shows came on the TV. Shows like The Stoneman Family, Porter Wagoner, The Wilburn Brothers *and* Lester Flatt & Earl Scruggs…*would captivate me for hours. Those shows formed my love for early country music, and it's still my favorite today. But at the same time, I still watch Lawrence Welk and love my Frank Sinatra and Tommy Dorsey records, along with all the '40s and '50s popular stuff—the stuff I grew up on. I always loved the radio, too, and would listen each Friday and Saturday nights to WSM's Grand Ole Opry. Best music on earth, and it's so sad that people don't even know what country music is today. Thank goodness that they kept a lot of the old radio transcripts of the early Opry shows, and WSM still plays them as part of the regular Saturday show today.*

He first heard the banjo played by an old woman who was his neighbor.

Pearl Ball was a local "character" in the Banjo Branch community and was without a doubt one of the finest old-time banjo players I've ever heard. Known as "Aunt Pearl" by people in the community (no relation to me) she was a valuable resource of the local history of the area, as well as being an incredible musician with a large repertoire of old and scarce tunes. Her banjo was one of the first sounds I heard when we moved up here in 1954. I visited her often as a child, and she became my "connection" and teacher to the old way of life (mountain culture, way of life, music, etc.) As far as I know, she was never formally recorded, which is a shame.

Roger has spent the past half century as a resident of Banjo Branch. According to Roger, this is how the area came to have the unusual name:

It seems at one time, many years ago, there was a big old house up the creek here where people would gather for "frolics" and dances. There was always a good supply of local moonshine, as well, and once in a while things there got "interesting." One night in particular, the banjo player and fiddler in the band had been sippin' quite a bit on the latest batch of spirits and were feeling no pain. At length, there was some sort of argument between the two, and they took the argument outside, where eventually the banjo player hit the fiddler over the head with his banjo. In those days, a banjo was just a hoop with a wooden stick run through it and a head stretched over it, so the head of the banjo broke off when it came down over the fiddler's head, and it rolled down the hill and plopped right into the branch. Other than the temporary loss of the music, no permanent injuries were noted. However, word of the incident spread, and soon thereafter the community where the fight had occurred was called "Banjo Branch," and the name stuck.

Roger is a self-taught musician. He was about eleven when his father bought him his first guitar. It was a Kay Value Leader 1 pickup electric, from his uncle Paul. Roger's father purchased it on a Sunday, and by Tuesday, the boy was playing all the chords. He used a Chet Atkins instruction book that came with the guitar, and the rhythm playing seemed to come naturally. Roger picked up technique from various people, but he taught himself how to play and still likes to finger pick. He said that this is probably a result of the early influence of the Chet Atkins book.

Everything I play is totally by ear, which is the traditional way everybody in the mountains plays their music anyway. People often ask me if I can read music, and I always say, "Not enough to mess up my playing." I believe that your ear is the most important part of playing, and the music has to be inside you and you have to know how to bring it out. This is the way it is with all the greats in traditional and country music, very few of them know or knew how to read music. So in the end, it's a gift I guess. I still practice from one to two hours per day, minimum, and it takes dedication and discipline like nothing else if you're going to be good at it. The ear cannot be ignored.

Roger has met many colorful characters and fine musicians from the hills of western North Carolina by attending festivals. He attended the first Bascom Lamar Lunsford Festival at Mars Hill College in 1967. That auditorium held 1,600, and there was nowhere to sit. So Roger stood up in the back near the doors. Roger had a little battery-operated cassette tape recorder that he hid under his jacket to tape most of the show. He was delighted to see all that talent up close for the first time. While Roger was still learning to play, his mother and father wanted their friends to come to the house just to hear him. The only way the little boy would consent to play was if he could go into his bedroom and shut the door. They could hear him without seeing him. Roger continued to practice and played with neighbors Charles Ball and Lloyd Ray, along with one of Charles's sons, Aaron. By the following year, Roger and Aaron were on the stage of the Lunsford Festival. Roger played the banjo, and Aaron played the guitar; they called themselves the Bailey Mountain Boys. That was one of his first stage performances, and Roger said, "I've been hooked ever since."

Thinking back on the early festival and meeting Lunsford and his wife, Frieda; Byard Ray; Tommy Hunter; and all the dancers, he said, "I thought I'd died and went to heaven." It was a very special memory.

Pearl Ball's nephew, Charles Ball (who lived just below us, and who played with me early on in the '60s) retired from a local manufacturing job and went to work at then Mars Hill College as a security guard. One night, during the Bascom Lamar Lunsford Festival (1970s), Mr. Lunsford[, who] was very elderly and unsteady[,] wanted to make an appearance at the show nevertheless. I was hanging out behind stage with Charles that night, and it was Charles's job to help "Mr. Bascom" up on stage and then back to the car afterward. I, of course, jumped at the chance to help, and after [I was introduced], Mr. Bascom found that I played the banjo, to which he said, "Well, that's fine, you keep that up. That's something that people want to hear!" We continued our discussion for a time, and Charles told him how I was learning a lot of the old banjo and fiddle tunes, to which Mr. Bascom smiled and shook my hand, and finally he drove away. I didn't get to speak to him much from then on, but he always remembered me, and that made me feel good, and I remember always taking his words seriously. It just made me feel special to shake his hand that night and have him speak so positively about my keeping up the old music. I guess he's someone that I've modeled myself after, when all is said and done.

Roger understands that North Carolina was a very big early influence in the shaping of what we hear now as bluegrass music. He feels that in other parts of the country the traditional sound of bluegrass is changing. He said:

It's a slicker, more homogenized form of the music, but hard-core North Carolina bluegrass contains all the necessary ingredients that it originally started with. I hope it resists the changes coming along in radio these days, but with the move of IBMA to Raleigh recently it's yet to be seen how the future artists and bands will move the genre forward. Many of the traditional early bluegrass artists that made Asheville one of the early bluegrass breeding grounds are dying out and being replaced by younger, more "progressive" players at an alarming rate. We seem to be at a "changing of the guard" when it comes to generations now, and I hope the younger folks will keep the early bluegrass style going. I fear it's dying out, though, right along with the early players and artists who made it what it is. So many young people from all over the world are flocking to Asheville's music scene these days, and it is naturally causing a lot of mixing in styles and genres, and I fear that true, authentic bluegrass music as we know it will change into something we won't recognize in another generation on out. All music is changing, though, it's not just bluegrass. Country music, as we knew it when I was growing up, isn't even played on the radio these days. So very sad. But I hope that enough young people will see the great importance in keeping bluegrass close to its roots and will stay the course. I know that there are an awful lot of young talented players who love the old ways of playing, and who are dead serious on keeping it alive. I guess time will tell.

Roger is proud of many of his accomplishments, the one that stands out the most is playing in and winning the competition for "Fiddler of the Festival" at Fiddler's Grove, one of the oldest continually operated festivals in the country. Many of his heroes and mentors have played at the festival and won the award. For Roger to win it in 2015 is a dream come true. He is also very proud of winning the Bascom Lunsford Award at the Mountain Dance & Folk Festival in Asheville in 2008 and at Mars Hill in 1999. Roger's winning of the Georgia State Championship on Banjo in 1995 at the Georgia Mountain Fair in Hiawassee, Georgia was also very special. This was the first time it was awarded to an "Old-Time" banjo player.

Roger has developed arthritis over the past few years, and it's taken its toll on his banjo playing and to some extent his guitar playing. He continues to keep hammering away at the guitar as much as possible and has found that when he stops playing the guitar and "gives in to the pain," it makes everything worse, including his fiddling, and that is not an option for Roger Howell. Instead he says:

I am forcing myself to play guitar every day and it's helping a lot. I want to do a new CD and am currently recording some stuff for that, and the new documentary film project that Mars Hill University is currently producing about me is kind of exciting. It is scheduled to premiere at the Bascom Lunsford Festival at the University in October, and will probably go nationwide soon thereafter. Who knows what opportunities that will open up? At my age, I do feel that I'm getting to the point where my music is being accepted as genuine and real and maybe something that people should have been looking at all along, especially from those in the regional and national arts level. I'm so grateful to still be able to physically get out and play, and I am having more fun right now than [at] any [other] time in my life with the music. I'm still learning things and new tunes every day, and I plan to keep playing until the very last thing I ever do. Think that's what I was put here for.

In 2013, Roger completed recording his impressive *Memory Collection of Fiddle Tunes.* These fiddle tunes, compiled for Mars Hill University's Southern Appalachian Archives, total 532 songs on twenty CDs. This collection has also been accepted at eight other major universities across the country.

Shindig on the Green
© 2012 Richard Hurley

Chorus:
Shindig, Shindig—Shindig on the Green—
Music, dancing—the best you've ever seen.

Saturday night in Asheville, that's the music scene—
Come on down and have some fun at the Shindig on the Green!
Arvil bows the fiddle; George he picks the "five";
Leonard plays the rhythm; Boyd keeps the beat alive.
They play for all the dance teams; been picking here for years;
Stoney Creek's the bluegrass band the people love to hear!
Folks come here to Asheville; they come from near and far
To hear a mountain banjo, a fiddle and guitar.
Glenn calls all the dances—he takes charge on the stage—
The sit-down and the street dance; you can clog at any age!

Chorus:
Shindig, Shindig—Shindig on the Green—
Youngsters, oldsters—like you've never seen.

The Lunsford stage is magic as the sunset paints the scene;
Bring your blanket; bring your chair to the Shindig on the Green!
There's BBQ a cookin' and ice cream if you please,

There's pickers on the courthouse steps and underneath the trees.
A few have won some Grammys in case you didn't know,
You can hear these big time pickers on the local bluegrass shows!
From July Fourth to Labor Day the folks all come to town
To join us at the Shindig along about sundown.
Here's to all the volunteers who keep our past alive
They're the reason all these years the Shindig has survived!

Chorus:
Shindig, Shindig—Shindig On The Green—
Music, dancing—the best you've ever seen.

Saturday night in Asheville, that's the music scene—
Come on down and have some fun at the Shindig on the Green!
Ah, sing one, Leonard!

For more information, including lineups and tickets, visit www.folkheritage.org.

RICHARD HURLEY

Richard grew up in Canton, North Carolina, in a house with music. His father, Jim, was from Rhode Island and sang in the church and played the tenor banjo a bit in the 1920s. He was an Ivy League graduate who worked as F. Scott Fitzgerald's personal secretary in Asheville in 1936 and learned to appreciate mountain and bluegrass music later in life. Richard's mother, Daisy, was an educated country girl who was self-proclaimed to be "tone deaf" and did not sing. There were some musicians in her family and her late brother, Albert Burnette, was a legendary storyteller and square dance caller. Richard said, "My older late brother, Jim Ab, played the washtub bass, and my younger brother, Pat, did vocals. We were influenced by Flatt & Scruggs, the Kingston Trio and similar groups from the folk era. The Trio was the major influence at that time, however. We simply called ourselves the Three Hurleys but mostly did living room concerts for home parties!"

The late Ed Pressley, a local guitar player who had a band in the '40s and '50s, opened a five-hundred-watt country music radio station WPTL in Canton in 1963. Pressley asked the senior English teacher at the local high school to recommend a teenager who could be a rock DJ to pull in the teen audience. He wanted to compete with the other local station that was playing the popular music of the day. Ed Pressley hired Richard to work daily after school at the station while he completed his senior year in high school. Richard recalls:

> I was making two dollars an hour and worked as an on-air personality playing country, bluegrass, gospel, rock and easy-listening music. A fellow DJ was the late Jimmy Haynie, who was a major influence on me as a kid since he did chapel programs at the local elementary schools. He was the National Folk Singing Champion in the '50s. In the '80s, he did an evening show at the Pisgah View Ranch and would call on me to fill in for him when he was ill or had another gig. After his death in 1987, I was offered the spot and did a family show every other Friday night for seventeen years.

The station had a faithful and dedicated audience. One memorable occasion was in 1968, when Richard was able to tape an original song and play it on the air at the station. The song was about local brothers who owned Smathers Market. This was one of Richard's first original songs. He said, "Ed granted my request to record it on an old eight-track radio spot cartridge and play it. It actually caught on and got some requests."

Richard has written many songs about his experiences growing up in western North Carolina and has always held a special place for the significance of the region, including the history rooted in the music of the mountains and the Scotch and Irish immigrants who moved in to the coves and hollers of Madison, Haywood, Buncombe and other neighboring counties in the 1700s. According to Richard:

> The "Father of Country Music," Jimmie Rodgers, supposedly got his start here in Asheville when he played on WWNC—the still prominent "Radio Voice of Western North Carolina." Bill Monroe and, I'm sure, many others played there sometime in the '40s and '50s. Becoming a bluegrass fan in the early '60s, I remember seeing Lester Flatt, Earl Scruggs and the Foggy Mountain Boys play the old City Auditorium in 1962 or thereabouts. Elvis had played there with Hank Snow in 1954, but the story was that the fans didn't care for his "music."

The legacy of great musicians from the region continues, and Richard could not be more proud of the long line of homegrown talent that has gained national prominence. He said:

Balsam Range's banjo player, Marc Pruett, who is also from Canton, won a Grammy on Ricky Skaggs's Bluegrass Rules *album, as did Bryan Sutton, a local guitar master who was named Guitar Player of the Year in 2014 for the eighth straight year by the IBMA. Legendary fiddler Bobby Hicks was on that album also and lives in Madison County. He's played with all the greats. Balsam Range won Bluegrass Band of the Year in 2014 and their tenor singer, Buddy Melton, was awarded Vocalist of the Year. At least one of the band's songs has received an award. Marc played banjo on my original song "Shindig on the Green." I've known their band members for years and have introduced them many times when doing my emcee thing. I've jammed some with Bryan and his talented dad, Jerry, but they are way out of my league as musicians!*

Richard does not consider himself to be a noted "bluegrass musician." However, a song he wrote in the late '70s, "The Ballad of Old Fort Mountain," was a collaboration with his old friend legendary banjo player Raymond Fairchild, Arvil Freeman—the patriarch of the old-time mountain fiddlers—and the Crowe Brothers, who joined in on bass and rhythm guitar. The song was recorded in 1981 and gained regional prominence.

Richard remains well known and respected on the local music scene and maintains friendships with a number of professional musicians, with whom he has collaborated over the years. In 2013, Richard recorded a fifteen-track CD of his original songs and music at Eddie Swann's studio, Regal Music. The banjo music on one CD track—"A Tribute to Bascom Lamar Lunsford"—was done by Josh Goforth, a local genius musician who tours with David Holt. Josh played the rhythm and lead guitars, the fiddle, the banjo, the mandolin and the bass as well as sang harmony vocals. He also created the arrangements and produced the album. David Holt, who toured with Doc Watson for fourteen years, served as an advisor. Richard said:

Personally, I felt good about the project and really loved working in the studio with Eddie Swann and Josh Goforth. Josh pulled in Chris Rosser to play piano, and Eddie pulled in Tony Creasman to provide some percussion work. Between the two of them, they have worked with James Taylor, Glen Campbell, Willie Nelson and other prominent artists. Recording the Old Fort song in 1981 with Eddie Swann, who owned the studio, and with Steven Heller—who produced Doc's Legacy Album and ran the console that day—would have to be a highlight in my music endeavors. We recorded it the old-fashioned way by gathering around a couple of mics, recording a few cuts, taking the best one and calling it a day!

Richard's CD *My Mountains, My Songs* has gained recognition by the North Carolina Society of Historians, and he received the organization's Paul Greene Award. He continues to be a champion for bluegrass in western North Carolina and acknowledges, in addition to those mentioned above, other musical influences to include Leonard Hollifield, mountain fiddler Roger Howell, the Stoney Creek Boys and Uncle Ted White and Whitewater Bluegrass. Richard's website is richardhurleymusic.com.

LARRY KLEIN

Most people in the bluegrass community know Larry Klein from his role as the associate producer of SCETV radio's *The Bluegrass Sound.* Larry has hosted the popular program for over twenty-five years. *The Bluegrass Sound* started in July 1983 on ETV radio and is a combination of traditional and contemporary bluegrass and old-time mountain music. Larry moved to Columbia, South Carolina, in 1987, and in addition to being a dermatologist-pathologist, Larry became the associate producer and host of *The Bluegrass Sound* in 1989. Ashley Carder, fellow musician and friend, said:

> *I first met Larry Klein sometime in the late 1980s. Larry and I first played music together as members of Bill Wells's band starting around 1992, and we have made music together off and on ever since. Larry has done so much to promote bluegrass music in South Carolina, especially through his efforts with his weekly radio show,* The Bluegrass Sound. *You won't meet a nicer person than Larry, and he is always ready to play some tunes with anyone he meets. I've thoroughly enjoyed knowing Larry through the years and will always treasure his friendship and the times we've shared in the music together, especially when we played in Bill Wells's band. He recently joined my band Palmetto Blue, and I'm looking forward to making music with Larry for many years to come.*

Between his time at Bill's Pickin' Parlor and the radio station, Larry had the opportunity to perform with Carolina legends, including Snuffy Jenkins, Pappy Sherrill and the Hired Hands. Larry plays a Dobro® guitar and sings. He has played, still plays with and has recorded with Willie Wells and the Blue Ridge Mountain Grass, Palmetto Blue, Amick Junction, Clarence Jackson, Pappy Sherrill and the Sherrill Family, the Flat Out Strangers and

Arnie Jones and the Black Bottom Biscuits. On any given Friday night, you can find Larry at Bill's Pickin' Parlor sitting up near the front stage with his friend Pat Ahrens.

On my visit to Bill's one Friday night, I watched Larry, smiling and applauding all the musicians who performed during the open stage program. He joked and laughed with his friends in the audience and heckled Willie Wells when Larry's raffle ticket number was not called. And when the performance was over, Larry grabbed his guitar and joined in with the large jam session taking place in the back room. Of all his personal and professional accomplishments, Larry said, "As a Dobro® player with Bill's group for over twenty years, some of my fondest musical memories were traveling up to the Carter Family Fold and performing."

In 2004, Larry received the South Carolina Jean Laney Harris Folk Heritage Advocacy Award from the South Carolina Arts Commission and legislature. Dr. Larry Klein is a South Carolina bluegrass champion and cherished member of the Pickin' Parlor family.

Ted Lehmann (His Story in His Words)

I'm seventy-four years old and have, truly, only been involved in bluegrass music for a little over a decade. I'm a child of World War II and graduated from high school in 1959. My earliest musical memories are [of] classical music and the operettas of Gilbert and Sullivan. My father was a great fan of Broadway shows, and the early LPs like *Oklahoma*, *South Pacific*, *Brigadoon* and others were around the house. Other early influences were the songs sung by the great bass singer Paul Robeson, who was a political activist with a strong tilt toward the left, and songs by the Almanac Singers, the early band that preceded the Weavers (Pete Seeger, Lee Hays and Fred Hellerman), who influenced my musical taste during the folk song craze of the '60s and '70s along with groups like the Kingston Trio, the Limelighters, Chad Mitchell Trio and others. I played and sang Oscar Brand's wonderful five LP set called *Bawdy Songs and Back Room Ballads*. While in high school, I also grew to love Frank Sinatra, Ella Fitzgerald, Dave Brubeck and a mostly forgotten but wonderfully torchy jazz singer named Chris Connor. I remember going to the Sunnybrook Ballroom in Pottstown, Pennsylvania, where we saw the Louis Armstrong All-Stars and the successor to the Glen Miller Orchestra. I wasn't much interested in rock, and *American Bandstand* was hardly on my screen.

CAROLINA BLUEGRASS

In college, I became increasingly interested in folk music, played the guitar and sang, as well as hung around Greenwich Village a little. Pete Seeger and Josh White were particularly interesting to me. I memorized and played the recording of Paul Robeson's "Ballad for Americans" for years, even combing Greenwich Village for another copy after I wore mine out. As it was not much sold in those days because Robeson was a communist, I had a hard time finding it, but an aunt of mine had a copy in her Manhattan apartment and gave it to me.

There followed a career teaching and a marriage in which my wife and I raised a couple of boys and moved from place to place as we followed my career. I retired in 1997, and we took to the road in a large fifth-wheel trailer, traveling to Civil War battle sites and to the West. We settled for a while in Myrtle Beach, where bluegrass hit us. I was beginning to think [that] I would like to start a blog but that I didn't have anything much to write about that anyone would have much interest in. In 2003, it was just an idea, but by December 2006, I realized we would be traveling a good deal once again, and I wanted a way to keep in touch with our kids and families, as well as leave a record of what we were doing. I had no idea it would ever be read by much of anyone else, but I wrote my first blog entry in late December 2006.

In late April 2003, we [had] attended Merlefest for the first time. By luck and a quick finger on the computer, I was able to buy excellent reserved seats at Main (Watson) Stage, which we still have, although we haven't been there in some years. We were introduced to all sorts of different kinds of music there, and I said, "So this is bluegrass!" While there, we met Cindy Baucom, one of the emcees and a syndicated radio host working out of Charlotte, who is also married to banjo master Terry Baucom. She told me we were at the beginning of a great adventure and would find bluegrass people to be hugely welcoming if they saw that we really liked the music. Little did she or we know how far that would go. A year later, I bought my first instrument, an inexpensive starter banjo, and started to learn to play.

Jennings Chestnut lived in a double-wide trailer just outside Conway, South Carolina, and owned a small, struggling music shop. We stopped into his shop one day to buy some instructional books or some sort of gear. I asked whether he did any teaching, and he said he didn't but would be glad to help me with my banjo when I ran into trouble. He helped me get the G-lick (the most basic banjo lick) on my way to absolute failure on the banjo. A year ago, I divorced my banjo and married a guitar. [I'm a] much happier man, now. Often, when we were hanging around his shop, someone would come through the door to visit with Jennings. He would say, "Ted's a Yankee, but he's OK"—high praise from the old southern gent.

Jennings ran a small yearly festival called Bluegrass on the Waccamaw in early May featuring a couple of good, traditional national bands and very good local talent. After a year or so, he invited us to work backstage as volunteers. It was back there [that] I first became really acquainted with the people in bluegrass bands. Irene worked with Miss Willie (Jennings's wife) on kitchen tasks while I did some hauling and carrying and took pictures, what I still do at festivals. We were off and running. The first entry in my blog from there is in May 2007, but Irene thinks we'd been going at least a year or more before that. Jennings introduced us to Chip Chipman, who has a music store in Moncks Corner, and to Guy and Tina's Pickin' Place, too.

We last saw Jennings Chestnut a few weeks before he died of cancer. We drove up to his double-wide in the country to find him outside on the lawn directing a delivery while his wife and daughter were in tears on the porch. It turns out he had ordered a casket from Walmart, saving thousands of dollars and behaving in an entirely characteristic fashion. When he died a few weeks later, he directed that he be driven to the cemetery with the casket in the back of "Old Blue," his old Chevy Suburban wagon. We often talk about this episode with Lynn and Brenda Butler from Anderson, South Carolina, who were friends of Jennings's. They introduced us to Darrell Adkins, the promoter of Musicians Against Childhood Cancer in Columbus, Ohio, where we were soon also volunteering. While there, we met Nashville's Grammy-winning singer/songwriter Carl Jackson, who, within a couple years, had me backstage doing photography for him at IBMA's Fan Fest. Through this, we met most of the heavy weights in bluegrass whom we had only seen from the audience before this. So Jennings turns out to have provided our most important entrée into the bluegrass world. Irene says I have the chronology wrong, but that's kind of it.

Tut Taylor, a native of Milledgeville, Georgia, lived in Wilkesboro, North Carolina, during the last years of his long and productive life. We met Tut in a pawn shop in Wilkesboro and ended up in his home for an interview. Tut had had a fabulous, if not lucrative, career playing the Dobro® in an unconventional fashion, playing with John Hartford on the Steam Powered Aereo Plain album. He died in April from old age and the effects of diabetes.

Dr. Bobby Jones was a general practice physician who lived in Shelby, North Carolina (near the birthplace of Earl Scruggs). He started his blog within a few months of when I started mine under the pseudonym Dr. Tom Bibey. After something of a dance, we finally met in Burlington at a festival. As these things go, we hit it off, as did our wives, and a friendship grew as our two blogs began. You can find his side of the story by looking at his blog (https://drtombibey.wordpress.com), which is still online, although he died of a brain tumor much too soon, almost three years ago [2012]. Don't believe anything he wrote about me. He wrote a good novel called *The Mandolin Case* while he was still healthy enough to write. We're sprinkled through each others' writing starting in 2007, and we finally met in 2008.

Through Bobby Jones, we met Darin Aldridge, a young bluegrass picker from Cherryville, North Carolina, and his then new fiancée, Brooke Justice, at a place called the Bomb Shelter in Cherryville. Darin and Brooke are now married, the sweethearts of bluegrass, and climbing up the ladder.

I've developed a little bit of a reputation, and Irene has found her own important niche, too. It's the best job I [have] ever had.

While bluegrass festivals vary enormously, there are probably a few constants because of the very nature of the music and its growth. The first multiday bluegrass festival was held over Labor Day weekend 1965 on Cantrell's horse farm near Fincastle, Virginia. It was promoted by Carlton Haney and included, among other performers, Bill Monroe and the Bluegrass Boys, Jimmy Martin, the Osborne Brothers, Don Reno and Red Smiley, Mac Wiseman and Doc Watson. An excellent account of the weekend and its impact can be found here. This happy event was attended by a strange mélange of local mountain people, hippies, northeastern folk singers, bluegrass musicians, bikers and assorted bluegrass fans. If you counted the number of people of a certain age who claim today they were there, the number of attendees would reach into the thousands. Probably the two essential elements found at almost every bluegrass festival are a main stage where professional bands perform and jam.

The majority of people at a bluegrass festival are there for the music and to socialize. Typically, festivals are outdoor affairs held in rural or semirural settings. They are sometimes found in established commercial campgrounds and some in venues called Music Parks. They are semi-developed settings with electric and water hookups, sometimes a shower building and a stage. We go to several festivals, some quite well-established older events held in what were, the day-before-yesterday, open fields that have been transformed into festival venues. Some of these have electricity, a big circus tent for the performance area, port-a-potties for the usual purposes and food vendors. Camping is usual, and people come with every conceivable kind of equipment from half-a-million-dollar buses through the full range of trailers to small tents. Some sleep in the back of their pickup trucks.

Many of the trucks have acoustic instruments in their rigs. The main tent is surrounded by vendors' rigs selling barbecue (southern gourmet), fried dough (southern fattening), kettle corn, fish, ice cream and crafts. There's usually a guy who sells flags, many of them you know. Vendors often include someone selling CDs, heavy on bluegrass but including some country music. A music supply vendor sells instructional materials, instruments, strings, picks, electronic tuners and much more. At pretty good-sized events, there are at least one and sometimes more high-quality luthiers selling quality instruments. This is what I call the movable community. Many of the people there know one another, attend many of the same events together and consider themselves to be close friends. As far as I know, these same friends may never have visited in one another's real homes. Fairgrounds, because they have pretty elaborate facilities, are good places for bluegrass promoters to select for festivals and are always looking for ways to get their facility used every weekend. I'm told that bluegrass festivals are well liked because we pretty much clean up after ourselves.

It's a little hard for me to tell how pervasive jamming is. Lots of people who love bluegrass play one (or more) of the standard bluegrass instruments: guitar, banjo, mandolin, fiddle, bass or Dobro®. They like to get them out and play together. Some jammers, like us, carry several instruments and jam some at festivals, mostly in the morning before the show starts, often around noon. Others jam after the show ends, say 10:00 or 11:00 p.m. and well into the night. Many festivals advertise that those who wish to can jam 24/7. Some festivals set aside quiet places where people who want to sleep without accompaniment can. And there's a subculture of jamming addicts who jam almost all the time and rarely go to the show unless a special friend of theirs or an unusually fine, in their estimation, band is playing. These people often see sunrise before heading for bed and are rarely seen before noon. Some of these serious jammers are superb musicians, often without the discipline or desire to play in touring bands, or they play in local and regional bands because they support themselves with straight jobs. They will, when cornered, describe themselves as addicts. They buy a ticket to the festival to get in but tend to camp in the free rough camping area most festivals provide, bringing their own food and drink. Most of these jams are pretty exclusive and woe befall the novice who carries a cheap banjo into their circle and tries to call a song. There are other jammers, mostly considerably older, who prefer to get together during the day to play classic country music. Incidentally, the old country songs are easier to play and sing than the kind of bluegrass invented by Bill Monroe, perfected by Flatt & Scruggs and widely played from the stage. I'd say the jamming community is essential to festivals and found to a greater or lesser extent everywhere.

The major change in my blog over time has been an increased interest in writing for the bluegrass "industry" while seeking to maintain a connection to grass-roots fans. I've been nominated for the IBMA Print/Media Person of the Year four times, never winning the award. I won't do sour grapes! I think that over time, I've become a better writer and photographer, learning more about telling stories, combining the two into what I guess could be called photojournalism. As I became more accomplished with video, I added my own videos to my blog entries, but while video supplies some small portion of my output, it actually consumes an inordinate amount of time at bluegrass festivals. Over time, I've come to see my blog as the cornerstone of a larger online presence that includes Facebook, Twitter and YouTube, as well as relevant listserves and forums, all focused on providing information and opinions about bluegrass. As the tenth anniversary approaches, it seems to me to be, in online terms, a well-established institution that could easily die in a single day. Meanwhile, I continue to try to grow and learn while maintaining a genial face toward those who read, contribute to and learn from what I write. One of my greatest joys, I must say, is walking through a festival ground or down an aisle in the audience and being greeted with a "Hi, Ted" by people I don't know.

Life's all a big web and stories are a huge part of it. I've worked too long on this and said way more than you need. You've been introduced to some of our favorite people, but lots more remain. Meanwhile, we've both found a fruitful life filled with friends we never even knew were there in 2003 when we embarked on this journey.

You can follow Ted's bluegrass at www.tedlehmann.blogspot.com. I'm sure you will agree he is a "good Yankee friend" and Carolina bluegrass champion. He also writes a weekly bluegrass column called "Bluegrass Rambles" for *No Depression*, an online alternative music e-zine.

THE STORY OF TONY McKIE

Home Team BBQ, Charleston, South Carolina

Home Team BBQ has built its brand on blues, bluegrass and Americana as played by national, regional and local touring artists with established schedules at reputable venues. It is encouraged that all artists have original, recorded compositions to promote.

STILL PICKIN' IN CAROLINA

Tony McKie has had a long relationship with traditional musicians in both jazz and blues, including Drink Small, the Blues Doctor. Tony said, "My 'relationship' with Drink Small started in 2007 and was encouraged and put together by Gary Erwin, aka Shrimp City Slim. Drink Small participated in what was then the Lowcountry Blues Bash, an event that was held at over seventeen venues over the course of ten days, featuring over 140 artists from around the world." Tony believes that informal "porch-step picking" brings out the natural talent some people are born with. Rural musicians can blossom from the lack of other activities and distraction, barring the twelve-plus-hour workdays that many people on farms work. Tony's connection to bluegrass began when he was in his late teens. He said:

> *Discovering the Grateful Dead and all the family fun associated with the three-night run…late night campfire drum circles were too much for even this drummer. Searching the campsite…meeting some nameless, faceless older hippies picking 'til dawn the tunes of Old & In The Way…was a religious experience. To this day…Jerry Garcia, David Grisman, Peter Rowan, Vassar Clements, John Kahn, Richard Greene, Herb Peterson and Bryn Bright are still my bluegrass heroes.*

From those early days, Tony has had a hand in creating the successful Home Team BBQ brand, and the Bar-B-Qued Bluegrass series is the newest incarnation of the old Thursday Night Series that featured a more traditional style limited to the Lowcountry. Originating at the now closed West Ashley Bait & Tackle (where the Tin Roof now operates at 1117 Magnolia Road), Thursday Night Bluegrass witnessed continued success and growth with the move to the new venue. For four years, it went strong, but as with most things that are done repetitively, enthusiasm started to wane. After a short rest, Home Team now hosts the three-night run, hosting two traveling bands and one local on three Tuesdays in a row, three times a year.

When it comes to the future of bluegrass, the best could be yet to come. According to Tony:

> *The future of bluegrass lives in the genes of such acts as Packway Handle Band, evident in their latest collaboration with Jim White. Alison Krauss, Del McCoury and Sam Bush continue to popularize the genre with festivalgoers and crossover fans. Travel to a mountain community (specifically Long Creek, South Carolina, comes to mind) and find music halls that still offer weekly free jams and get togethers. Bluegrass will remain strong. It too has its own XM channel.*

Palmetto Blue

The band photograph was taken on a clear November day. Everyone was dressed in color-coordinated jackets or sweaters, and one young woman sat perched on a hay bale, giving the traditional bluegrass touch. It's such a calm portrait you can just about hear the whippoorwills in the woods. In many ways, the picture looks like a family portrait. Steve Willis, Ashley Carder, Anna Davis Cumbee, Chris Boutwell and Shellie Davis might not all be related, but they are a great example of a tightknit bluegrass band made up family members and friends. Palmetto Blue has become one of the most well-respected bands in the area.

According to Ashley Carder:

> We started our band Palmetto Blue in the summer of 2013 and have been really busy ever since. We've played at the South Carolina State Fair, the South Carolina State Museum, USC McKissick Museum's FOLKFabulous Festival, the Forest Acres Festival, the St. Patrick's Day Festival in Five Points, the Tasty Tomato Festival, the Fiftieth Annual National Convention of the U.S. Special Forces and Green Berets, the International Oak Society and many regional festivals and venues, as well as private parties, weddings, churches, etc.

Palmetto Blue. *From left to right*: Steve Willis (banjo), Ashley Carder (fiddle), Anna Davis Cumbee (guitar), Chris Boutwell (mandolin) and Shellie Davis (bass). *Courtesy of Ashley Carder.*

The group consists of well-established musicians and talented newcomers, the next generation of pickers. Dr. Larry Klein joined the group in the summer of 2015; now there are three South Carolina Folk Heritage award recipients in the band: Larry, Chris and Ashley.

David Prosser, the Carolina Rebels

David Prosser was always interested in music, and by the age of eleven, he was learning to play the guitar. At that time, he assumed he would play rock 'n' roll, although he didn't enjoy playing rock 'n' roll. David found something he did enjoy playing a few years later. When David was sixteen, he and his best friend, Don, started cutting grass and doing odd jobs for extra spending money. One rainy day, the boys were stuck in the house, and David decided to pull out some of the family albums. The first album was Flatt and Scruggs, and the title song on the album was the original "Foggy Mountain Breakdown." It was raining outside; inside the house, the music hit the teenagers like a bolt of lightning. David said, "I was hooked, so was Don. He fell for the fiddle, but for me, it was the banjo."

The boys spent two weeks working hard to raise money to buy their respective instruments. They spent the rest of the summer trying to learn to play. David's father, Julian "Hank" Prosser, told the boys that if they learned to play, he would put a bluegrass band together. The idea of being in a bluegrass band inspired the young men to spend the entire year focused on mastering their instruments until they finally got it down. By the end of the school year, David's dad said, "OK, boys, I think you're ready."

Mr. Prosser spoke to a neighbor and friend, Tom Sherrod, who lived down the street. Tom was a good singer. Soon they all started practicing together with bass player Bob Dockery. They called themselves the Carolina Rebels, and they still play together today. Although Bob has since retired, Tom and Hank still play with the band and have been joined by Burle Rodgerson.

Good times and good memories—and some pretty funny memories at that—have followed. There was never a dull moment when his friend Little Roy Lewis would join them on stage. Their group would have fun picking on other bands. For example, someone would dress up as a cow and hop on stage when another band played "Milk Cow Blues." Or somebody would ask the sound man to turn off the banjo microphone on stage and turn it on for David backstage. When the break came, it would be David who would play. The band onstage would be baffled and confused, and the audience would roar with laughter as David played on and on.

According to David, "North and South Carolina have spawned some of the first generation of greats: Earl Scruggs, Don Reno, Snuffy Jenkins, Carl Story and Bill Haney, just to name a few. [And they boast] the second, third and fourth generations of Randy Lucas, Kristy Scott Benson and, of course you can't forget, Terry Baucom. The Carolinas have always had a huge input on bluegrass music and continue to do so."

David acknowledges how the music has grown from the first "band" of Earl Scruggs, Lester Flatt, Chubby Wise, Bill Monroe and Cedric Rainwater. He believes that the music was already something that was going to grow and change and said:

> We have seen Earl and Lester expand the music, bringing in folk music, then groups like the Earl Scruggs Review and the New Grass Revival, rock and even reggae into the music. I would hope that the music continues to move in multiple directions. Today, young people are finding the traditional roots and holding on to them as well as expanding and adding new things to the music, maybe more classical and jazz. There are already some Dixieland sounds. Adding more would only let the music grow.

If David could go back to 1979, he would give himself some advice:

> I'd tell myself to relax and not fight the instrument as much as I did the first few months I was learning to play. It took me a couple months to break myself of bad habits I formed in playing, and I would have gotten much farther faster if I had not fought with the instrument. Also, I think I would have said, "Listen to your dad because he knows more about the music than you think."

THE CAROLINA ROSE

Bluegrass songs with their stories of heartbreak and sadness have been called "a celebration of pain." It's not uncommon to find songs that include descriptive lyrics about dying soldiers, sick mothers, wayfaring children and tragic train wrecks. These old-time melodies of misery have been featured in Broadway plays such as *Bright Star* by Steve Martin and Edie Brickell (2015), as well as on the big screen as in *O Brother, Where Art Thou* by the

Coen brothers (2000). If California agent, producer and distributor William E. Bales and scriptwriter Jordan River of Stars of Hollywood Network (StarsofHollywoodNetwork.com) have their way, another bluegrass story will be coming soon to a theater near you.

Shirley Landsdown was promoting the music of Carolina Rose through social media. Rose asked her to become her manager, and for the past two years, Landsdown travels with Carolina Rose, takes promotional and fan photographs and records some videos for the North Carolina traditional bluegrass guitarist. The two have been working with William E. Bales and Jordan Rivers on a film they believe will "set the historical record straight." However, making a feature film is time consuming and expensive, and the process has been slow. Carolina Rose has a complicated life story, one that she has already shared in her autobiography, *The Road from Gloria Jean to Carolina Rose*. Carolina Rose, country music turned bluegrass singer-songwriter and guitarist, has set the opening scene with an original song she performs at all her concerts.

I was born in Carolina
Way down where the tall pines grow
Way down in ole Carolina
They call me Carolina Rose.
My mother left me with another
A carefree life she had chose
Now I've grown into a woman
I'm the one my mother couldn't stand.

Chorus:
When I was born
She didn't want me
She gave me away that very day
Two weeks later came back and took me
carried me to Norwood and again gave me away.

Chorus

When I'd ask her who is my Father
She wouldn't tell me his name
SHE HATED HIM, SHE HATED ME
She'd say, "It's in your genes girl, you were born to sing"

As the story goes, during the early days of bluegrass, bands seeking to make a name for themselves would spend weeks and even months on the road. They traveled to small towns, county fairs and community concerts. The musicians were accessible to their fans, and wives understood the old saying, "A handsome husband is common property." Many wives would travel along with the band and sit on the stage where they could keep a watchful eye on the crowd and their men. Other married men made it a point to do the show and get out of town as soon as possible. If the musician wasn't married? That was another story altogether.

Everyone in the sleepy town of Norwood, North Carolina, looked forward to entertainment provided by musicians playing their favorite old-time music. The music, dancing and parties attracted young and old alike.

On one such occasion in 1943, Ruby Elma Polk met a broad-shouldered, good-looking, up-and-coming young mandolin player. This fellow dressed more like a banker than a musician, and as Carolina Rose explained, he wasn't famous or married. The concert was under the big tent on the schoolyard grounds. Young people from Norwood and the surrounding areas could hardly wait to let the good times roll. Well, as the saying goes, you can't put old heads on young shoulders. Ruby Elma was twenty-four years old and swept off her feet by the handsome, fancy-dressed man on stage that night. Months after the concert, less than a year later, she gave birth to her first child, Gloria Jean Polk (aka Carolina Rose). The young mother made the decision to give her firstborn child up for adoption. Her family, however, insisted that the child would not be raised by strangers, and little Gloria Jean was brought back home.

When the baby was two weeks old, she was given to Ruby Elma's sister Virgie to raise. Virgie was happily married to Eunie Hilliard and lived a comfortable lifestyle. Virgie and Eunie raised the child as if she were their own until tragedy struck six years later. Eunie and his brother-in-law were killed in an automobile accident that devastated the family. In 1950, Virgie remarried a well-to-do gentleman named James G. Johnson. The couple were devoted to each other and showered little Gloria Jean with love and attention.

In a 2013 interview with Christian Lamiskcha, publisher of *Country Music News International*, Carolina Rose said: "I was given to Virgie Polk Johnson and her husband James Johnson by my biological mother when I was two weeks old. They raised me as their own and I had a wonderful childhood. My mom [Virgie] always took time for anything I needed or wanted. She was always there to help me."

Ruby Elma had very little to do with the child who looked more and more like her biological father every year. Things were not always easy, and Gloria Jean learned early on how to ignore the hushed whispers and small-town gossip. Gloria Jean began singing at about seven or eight years old, and Virgie ordered her first guitar from Sears and Roebuck. Gloria Jean loved the music of Bill Monroe and the Bluegrass Boys. Carolina Rose said, "My mom that raised me was a big inspiration because she always took time to carry me anywhere for my music." Gloria Jean was talented and received help along the way. She met Martha Carson, the "First Lady of Gospel Music," and had the opportunity to tour with Roni Stoneman, the "First Lady of Banjo."

Ruby Elma Polk married and had seven children, and the distance between mother and first daughter grew wider.

In 1963, Gloria Jean married Harold Dunlap Harward, and the couple had four children. The marriage unfortunately did not last, and they divorced in the mid-'70s.

Carolina Rose was searching for more information about her family history. In a conversation with first cousin Billy Wayne Hargett, a respected deacon in the church, the identity of her biological father was finally revealed. As the years passed and Ruby Elma's health was declining, Carolina Rose met with her, and the two women made peace. Ruby Elma passed away, as did Virgie and James.

Carolina Rose continues to perform her traditional show with the Bluegrass Girls. The ladies always dress the part, and she wears her trademark red cowgirl hat.

Back in Norwood, people have not been a bit surprised about the ballad of little Gloria Jean.

A newspaper reporter who wrote a story about the film told me, "[For] folks around Norwood, well it [who her famous biological father is] is a known fact here, and she really looks just like him."

Manager Shirley Landsdown is excited about the upcoming film and said, "In essence, I have known Carolina Rose going on two years. She is a fantastic songwriter and entertainer in my book; she is one of the best in her field. She has lots of things coming up in the next few months. Two I can mention is this book, and then she is going to Jerusalem Ridge again in September. "

Carolina Rose has been featured as one of the treasured bands at the Jerusalem Ridge Festival for more than thirteen consecutive years. The popular event is held on the land where legendary mandolin player Bill Monroe was born and raised.

What does Carolina Rose want? According to the 2013 *Country Music News International* magazine interview, she said, "My hopes and deep desire is [*sic*] to be able to perform for a long time to come, to be happy because sometimes it is very hard to be happy in today's world."

As you can see, the ballad of little Gloria Jean is complicated. But you never know: the movie produced by the Stars of Hollywood Network could be just what's needed to make sure everything turns out right.

"Uncle" Ted White

I really hope you get it right because the academics keep getting it wrong. We weren't worried about playing bluegrass or old time or Celtic. We were playing music.
—*Ted White*

Ted's father was a textile man, and in the early 1960s, he was working for Reeves Brothers Mill in Cornelius, North Carolina. The family was living in Mooresville, North Carolina, at the time. His father was a wonderful clarinet and piano player and had actually played on *The Perry Como Show*. His mother was originally from Spartanburg, South Carolina, and she read music and played the piano. Ted said, "My mother thought the only person who could bring children into this world was Dr. John Flemming, so all of us were born in Spartanburg, South Carolina. Dr. John brought me into this world and gave me my first drink of liquor, but not on the same day."

Reeves Brothers did all the foam and fabric work for the automobiles coming out of Detroit. There was nothing exciting about living in a small textile town, so Ted said his father wanted to make a concession to his mother; he bought her a piano. The day it arrived, his mother was overjoyed. "She could read music, but she just couldn't keep time," Ted said. His mother played all afternoon out of the Presbyterian Hymnal, and Ted and his siblings "just suffered through it." When his father got home, he was so excited to hear the piano through the window that he rushed in, threw his coat on the couch, rolled up his sleeves and sat down to play the boogie woogie. The neighbors were so excited to hear him play that they came up on the porch to listen through the open windows.

By 1972, the family was back in Asheville, North Carolina, and for Christmas that year, Ted's parents bought him a guitar. He said, "It was the best gift I ever received from my parents." Western North Carolina was a hot bed for talented musicians from all different genres of music, including Grammy Award–winning artists Warren Haynes (the Allman Brothers

Band, Gov't Mule and the Grateful Dead) Marc Pruett (Balsam Range), David Holt, Cornell Proctor (Triadstone Choir) and Billy Edd Wheeler (Songwriter of "Jackson" for Johnny Cash and June Carter Cash), to name just a few. There was great music everywhere.

In January 1973, Ted was trying to earn money for a Boy Scout trip coming up in July. A new Ingles supermarket was being built on Charlotte Street in Asheville. Ted went by every afternoon to ask for a job. Finally, Ernie Pressley, the manager, said he would give Ted a job, but first he had to get the store built. Ted said, "Well, can you put me somewhere to train so I'll be ready when you open?" Mr. Pressley put Ted out at the Ingles store on Merrimon Avenue sweeping up after the butcher. The butcher was a gruff man who barely spoke to Ted. "He only taught me to make coffee so he could complain about it," Ted said.

Sometime in February, Mark Davis, son of John Davis of Asheville bluegrass fame, saw Ted at school and invited him to a jam session at his father's house on Chatam Road. When Ted walked through the door he looked over and said, "Well, there's Arvil Freeman, the butcher!" The room fell quiet, and John looked at Ted and said, "The butcher—hell, that's the finest fiddle player in the Southeast. Come in, sit down and try to learn something."

Arvil Freeman had been playing professionally since he was fourteen years old. Over the years, he played with the Green Valley Boys at the radio station WCYB in Bristol, Tennessee, and had been offered a job with bluegrass stars Bill Monroe and the Stanley Brothers. Ted explained that the men jamming in the little house were so in demand that they would work their ten-hour days, four days a week and then travel to Nashville, where they would have gigs on Friday and Saturday nights. If Ted could go back and do it all over again, he would have paid even closer attention and taken it all in. Today, he understands what an amazing education he was getting "in that little house on Chatam Road." He said, "These men were wonderful stewards of the music. Arvil Freeman was the guy! I was so intimidated by the music they were playing. I didn't want to take my guitar out of the case. We were just a couple of raggedy boys tryin' to learn this music."

Ted did learn, and he learned the hard way sometimes. When one mentor, Paul Crouch, also known as the "fiddling fireman," wanted Ted to play the Lester Flatt G-run, he had Ted stand beside him, and when he wanted the run, he would swing his elbow out and hit Ted in the jaw. "I still can't play that run without my jaw hurting," Ted said.

Ted is also a third-generation square dance caller in his family. Since 1981, he and his business partner, Bill Byerly, have been the co-owners of the band the Whitewater Bluegrass Company. Because he is a square dance caller, the band has concentrated its work doing corporate events and wedding rehearsal dinners and receptions, as well as a few festivals. The band does between 130 and 150 dates a year. "We are listed with six agencies, and we do a lot of our own booking. You may not get famous picking with us, but you won't go hungry," Ted said.

The North Carolina Heritage Award

The North Carolina Arts Council Heritage awards are given in recognition of traditional artists. Recipients of the Heritage Awards range from internationally acclaimed musicians to individuals who continue to practice their art in rural and family settings. The Heritage Award has become one of the most important and influential programs developed by the Folklife Program of the North Carolina Arts Council. Thank you Sarah Bryan for helping to compile this information. Bluegrass and traditional winners of the award are listed:

1989

Tommy Hunter, fiddler
Doug Wallin, ballad singer
Etta Baker, old-time musician, banjo player and guitarist

1990

Badgett Sisters, gospel singers
Walker Calhoun, Cherokee tradition bearer and old-time banjo player
Earnest East, fiddler
Benton Flippen, fiddler
Dellie Norton, ballad singer

STILL PICKIN' IN CAROLINA

1991

The Menhaden Shantymen, work song singers
Quay Smathers, shape-note singing leader
Joe and Odell Thompson, string band musicians

1992

Bertie Dickens, banjo player
Leonard Glenn, banjo and dulcimer maker, old-time musician
Lauchlin Shaw and A.C. Overton, fiddler and banjo player

1993

Mary Jane Queen, ballad singer and banjo player
Luke and Harold Smathers, string band musicians

1994

Carroll Best, banjo player
Robert and Myrtle Dotson, old-time flatfoot dancers
The Watson Family (Doc, Rosa Lee, R. J., Arnold, Willard and Ora Watson),
old-time musicians

1995

Jim Shumate, fiddler
Ora Watson, fiddler (different Ora Watson from the one who was recognized
with the Watson Family)

CAROLINA BLUEGRASS

1996

Doc Rmah, Montagnard musician
Verlen Clifton and Paul Sutphin, string band musicians
Earl Scruggs

1998

Bessie Killens Eldreth, ballad singer
Smith McInnis, fiddler
Arthur "Guitar Boogie" Smith, string band musician
The Wilson Brothers, gospel bluegrass duo

2000

Marvin Gaster, banjo player and fiddler
Bobby McMillon, storyteller and ballad singer

2003

Bishop Dready Manning, gospel musician and composer
The Briarhoppers, string band
Oscar "Red" Wilson, string band musician

2007

George Shuffler, guitarist

2014

Bobby Hicks, fiddler

The South Carolina Jean Laney Harris Folk Heritage Award

The South Carolina Folk Heritage Award was created by the South Carolina Legislature in 1987 to recognize lifetime achievement in the traditional arts. In 1997, the name was changed to the Jean Laney Harris Folk Heritage Award in memory of state representative Harris's longtime support of South Carolina's cultural heritage. Along with the Elizabeth O'Neill Verner Governor's Award for the Arts, the Jean Laney Harris Folk Heritage Award is part of the South Carolina Arts Award Program. The McKissick Museum and the South Carolina Arts Commission administer the awards process. Winners of the award are:

1988: DeWitt "Snuffy" Jenkins and Homer "Pappy" Sherrill, bluegrass and old-time country music
1992: The Lucas Family, bluegrass and old-time country music
1995: Roger Bellow, advocacy and old-time country music
1996: Pat Ahrens, advocacy and bluegrass music
1998: Bill Wells, advocacy and bluegrass music
1997: Clarence Jackson, old-time county and bluegrass music
2000: J.C. Owens, old-time fiddling
2002: Jennings Chestnut Sr., advocacy and bluegrass music
2004: Larry Klein, advocacy and bluegrass music
2004: Ted Brackett, old-time fiddling
2005: Charles Summer, old-time fiddling
2006: T.C. Foster, old-time fiddling
2006: Guy and Tina Faulk, advocacy and bluegrass music
2008: Richard "Chip" Chipman, advocacy and bluegrass music
2012: Ashley Carder, fiddle music
2014: Chris Boutwell, bluegrass music

A Carolina Treasure

The Old-Time Herald *(OTH) Magazine*

Special thanks to Sarah Bryan for providing the following information about the *OTH*, as well as her personal American roots music story.

CAROLINA BLUEGRASS

The *Old-Time Herald* magazine was founded in 1987 by the pioneering old-time and bluegrass musician Alice Gerrard. Originally based in Galax, Virginia, its home base has been Durham, North Carolina, for many years. The *OTH*, which is published by the nonprofit Old-Time Music Group, covers the pre-bluegrass string band music of Appalachia and the Southeast, as well as related styles, including the old-time string band music of other regions of the country, ballad singing and traditional blues and gospel. In 2008, when editor Gail Gillespie (who succeeded Alice Gerrard) retired, I became the editor. I'm very proud of the stories and photography that the *Old-Time Herald* has carried in its nearly thirty years of publication. We feature articles about elder tradition bearers, historic artists of early country music and the younger people who have carried old-time music traditions into the future, as well as reviews, news about old-time music and commentary from our readers. The *Old-Time Herald* has subscribers in nearly every state in the nation and in Canada, throughout Europe and in Japan.

I'm originally from Myrtle Beach, South Carolina, with family roots in Horry County, South Carolina; throughout North Carolina; and Havana, Cuba. Some of my ancestors in Piedmont North Carolina were old-time musicians (playing autoharp, piano and guitar and singing shaped-note hymns), but I would describe myself as a revivalist, having been introduced to traditional music by artists who themselves came to the tradition through the old-time music revival. As a teenager, while living in northern Virginia, I had the good fortune to take fiddle and banjo lessons for three years from Bruce Molsky, and I've been playing ever since. Though I've played for square dances and appeared on *A Prairie Home Companion*, I prefer playing music informally with my husband and with friends to performing publicly. My husband, Peter Honig, is an old-time fiddler and guitar player, and we're both collectors of early 78 rpm records of string band music and other styles. We live in Durham, North Carolina. In addition to editing the *Old-Time Herald*, I work as a folklorist and have worked throughout the Carolinas documenting the music, craft, oral history and occupational traditions of the region.

Those interested can learn more about the magazine at oldtimeherald.org.

A Brief History of the South Carolina Bluegrass and Traditional Music Association (SC BTMA)

Provided by Pat Ahrens

The SC BMTA was co-founded by the late Bill Wells and Pat Ahrens in 1991. It is a nonprofit organization chartered by the state. Its primary objectives are to preserve, promote, publicize and support this unique musical style through concerts, workshops and public education programs.

The association decided to go inactive in 2006 but was reactivated in 2014. Founding members were Bill Wells, president; Pat Ahrens, vice-president; Susan Coleman, secretary; Terry Murphy, treasurer; and board of directors members Pappy Sherrill, Claude Lucas, Dr. Larry Klein, Frank Stover, Lester Gantt and Joan Davis.

Joe Wise and the Caroline Boys, WBLR *Ridge Jamboree*. Johnny Fenlayson on Banjo. *Courtesy of Ashley Carder.*

There are two people who deserve special mention for their hard work in establishing the bylaws and obtaining the organization's 501(c)3 status: Frank Stover and Terry Murphy. Jim Grey edited the newsletters for a long time. The association has a proud history of presenting this music to the public in many different ways.

Columbia, South Carolina concert featuring Johnny Cash. *Courtesy of Pat Ahrens.*

STILL PICKIN' IN CAROLINA

Selected Quotes and Memories

In collecting stories for this book, there were moments when people said such interesting and beautiful things about bluegrass music and the community that I want to include them in a special tribute section. Enjoy!

To me, bluegrass just has a depth to it that a lot of other music, especially current music today, lacks.

—*Bailee Lucas*

Oh, you have a good time playing music, but things happen that let you know you have a real responsibility to your audience. What you present to them, whether it's your song material or the way you conduct yourself, is weighty. This was brought home to me in hair-raising fashion when on a couple of different occasions I've been told that because that person and, later, another person heard a song of mine on the radio just as they were about to jump off that bridge or drive off that road into a tree, and it made them change their minds. When someone tells you something like that, it's an incredibly humbling experience, and you never again look at what you do in the same light.

—*Martha Adcock*

Then you just let the music carry you on and the people love it, and there's no better feeling in the world than being up on stage playing your instrument. I guess it's like they say, "You don't choose to play music, but music chooses you." At least, that's the way it is with me.

—*Roger Howell*

My first memory of a bluegrass festival was in Lavonia, Georgia. There was a creek behind the stage, and I played in the water, more than anything else. I'm guessing I was five years old. It was largely like bluegrass festivals still are today, a very safe environment and my parents were able to sit in the concert area and keep an eye on me while they listened to the music. I do remember being very impressed by the band, the Johnson Mountain Boys. They were relatively new to the scene and absolutely killed the audience that day. Even as a kid, I recognized their enthusiasm and realized that they were great.

—*Kristin Scott Benson*

Jim and Jenny's was the first bluegrass festival I remember attending. It was in the mountains of North Carolina, and the first band I was ever in, called Fret High, played it. The lineup was all regional bands, and I was about fifteen years old, at the time.

—Wayne Benson

I've been fortunate to have been all over the world, but there's no place like North Carolina and South Carolina to me. I lived in North Carolina my first twenty-eight years and lived in South Carolina the last twenty-two years. I'm very fortunate to have grown up in this mecca of acoustic music and have had the opportunity to hear all the great musicians from these states.

—Alan Bibey

In the spring of 2002, I think, we were in Myrtle Beach and heard that the Rivertown Bluegrass Society in Conway had monthly meetings with live music. We went one night where Alan Bibey and his very fine band BlueRidge would be performing. The music was fast, Bibey a mandolin virtuoso, and we were struck. We started attending local events and listening to the music. The next spring, we attended Merlefest in Wilkesboro, North Carolina, and it all changed. We heard Doc Watson, Sam Bush, Jerry Douglas and many more bands over a magical four-day period, and our lives were changed.

—Ted Lehmann

Many feel Bluegrass has to "stay the same"—utilizing the same five or six instruments—or they act like you have violated some kind of law printed somewhere. I look at bluegrass just like I look at a tree: it has to have healthy roots...but, it also has to be allowed to branch out and grow...or it dies.

—Cindy Baucom

Hopefully in fifty years, bluegrass will sound exactly the same. In a world full of auto tune and digital touch-ups, bluegrass stands out as delightfully imperfect and totally spontaneous.

—Jim Graddick

I think a lot of people fail to realize that if you are going to the Cherokee, North Carolina bluegrass festival, you are going to see families who have had the same camping spot for twenty years. If the festival starts on Thursday, they are going to leave their house Wednesday morning at 10:00 a.m., and they are going to eat at the Huddle House or I-Hop, whatever they like. They are going to fill their motorhome at Exit 74, back up into their camping space and set their stuff up. That kind of tradition is part of the music.

—*Wayne Benson*

My first favorite [performer] was Bill Monroe and the Bluegrass Boys. At that time I did not know names but loved the music. Some years later I found that Bill was the Father and Founder of Bluegrass. Without this man we would not have Bluegrass Music. He was a fantastic songwriter. All his songs are sung from the heart. He made the Mandolin talk as the saying goes. He was a very sharp dresser and he made the band dress that way. I was able to meet Bill Monroe in person, he was an awesome person and down to earth and kind spoken.

—*Shirley Landsdown*

Since we have so many young (like 8 and up) kids around here who are being prompted by their parents, I think we will see a perpetuation of song, music and dance for years to come. Maybe in twenty years, some of my songs will get sung at a Shindig program of the Folk Festival. That would be a tremendous legacy to leave behind! However, I hope I have my mother's genes and live to be nearly 101.

—*Richard Hurley*

In my experience bluegrass music is more culturally defined; therefore, those who actually relate to it are drawn together.

—*Randy Lucas*

The most valuable things I have? My fiddle, my grandfather's guitar and our family's pictures.

—*Jim Graddick*

In my opinion, my lifelong passion was racing, southern stock car racing, at the ol' Historic Columbia Speedway. Nascar and local dirt track racing. I have met many "superstars" of the sport. I have [driven] on dirt and asphalt tracks. When I decided to stop racing in 2001, I just messed around the house and our little farm south of Cayce, just piddlin' around. Then one morning, I woke up and told my wife I was goin' to buy a mandolin and play bluegrass, and she thought I had fell out of bed and hit

Early South Carolina Congaree Bluegrass Festival memorabilia. *Courtesy of Pat Ahrens.*

my head. I soon met the late Bill Wells, and he [advised] me [to learn] the guitar first. So I bought my first real guitar from Bill and took lessons from his teacher.

—Danny Creamer

The first time I ever played bluegrass was at Bill's Pickin Parlor. I was talked into going by Jim Graddick and was asked to play with nearly every group going on stage for [the] open mic within fifteen minutes of coming in the door. I was clueless as to what I was doing, and it was probably embarrassingly bad. But I had a great time and met lots of great people.

—Katie Miller

You will find car mechanics, doctors, lawyers, students, farmers and all kinds of people here [Bill's Pickin' Parlor], and I hope it is still here twenty years from now. Bill Wells had a vision, no electric musician, a place to promote traditional music, old-time stuff. That's what makes it so special.

—Ashley Carder

STILL PICKIN' IN CAROLINA

Friday at the Pickin' Parlor
© 2014, Ashley Carder

Instrumental intro
He came from old Virginia, in the green and rolling hills.
He sang and played the guitar, and we called him Mr. Bill.
Bluegrass music was his passion, and he played it all his life.
He moved to South Carolina, home of Miss Louise, his wife.
He began the pickin' parlor and he opened up the doors.
People came from far and wide to come and jam out on the floor.
Friday night became a happy time for pickers young and old.
Grandpas with hair of silver jammed with kids with hair of gold.
Come on and get up on the stage and play your favorite song
Then gather in a circle, and jam the whole night long
You'll hear guitars, you'll hear banjos, people sawing fiddles too.
Friday at the Pickin' Parlor where the grass is always blue
There was Mr. MJ Holden, there was Dr. Larry Klein
They made their Dobros ^R *sing and made them sound so very fine.*
Harold Lucas played the guitar, Pappy Sherrill sawed the strings.
Snuffy Jenkins played the washboard and could make the banjo ring.
Miss Pat would run the open stage, bring folks up from the floor.
Ralph Cox would play his guitar with fiddlin' Jim and many more.
There was Jack with his cowboy songs and Claude's Old Grey Mule.
For the kids who paid attention it was like a bluegrass school.

Chorus:
Come on and get up on the stage and play your favorite song
Then gather in a circle, and jam the whole night long
You'll hear mandolins and Dobros ^R*, and the big bass fiddle too.*
Friday at the Pickin' Parlor where the grass is always blue

It felt just like the Opry when you stepped up on the stage
Where Ralph Stanley's played his songs, so has Rhonda and the Rage.
The boys of Sugarloaf Mountain, Shellie and Palmetto Blue,
Vernon Riddle and his fiddle, Jeremy Johnson singing too.
People from all walks of life, they meet like family.
Doctor, farmer, lawyer, student, we're all the same you see.
Bill brought us all together through this music that we love.
Good ol' bluegrass music, that's what we're speaking of.

Bill's Music Shop, West Columbia, South Carolina. *Courtesy of Willie Wells.*

Chorus:
Come on and get up on the stage and play your favorite song.
Then gather in a circle, and jam the whole night long.
You'll hear high and lonesome singing and an old hoedown or two.
Friday at the Pickin' Parlor where the grass is always blue.

Bill Wells, he gave us all a home for oh so many years.
When Mr. Bill, he left us, we all shed many tears.
But Willie's carrying on the place and we still have Miss Pat,
And we think of Mr. Bill each time we see his hat.
Many who've been on his stage are now up there with Bill
Now over that Golden Shore we know they're picking still.
But with Ella, Reece, Worth, Shellie, Anna, and the Speares.
The music that Bill loved is in good hands for many years.

Chorus:
Come on and get up on the stage and play your favorite song.
Then gather in a circle, and jam the whole night long.
You'll hear guitars, you'll hear banjos, people sawing fiddles too.
Friday at the Pickin' Parlor where the grass is always blue.
Friday at the Pickin' Parlor where the grass (where the grass, where the grass)
Is always blue.

M.J. Holden, Dave Holder and others on a Friday night at Bill's Pickin' Parlor. *Courtesy of Bill's Music Shop & Pickin' Parlor.*

Greg Cahill and the Special Consensus. *Courtesy of Bill's Music Shop & Pickin' Parlor.*

BOBBY HICKS

I've been friends with Bobby Hicks for a long time and always admired his musicianship…from his work with Bill Monroe up until now. I got to record with him on the original recordings of Doyle Lawson & Quicksilver, and we toured together in the early 1980s with the Bluegrass Album Band. That gave me a glimpse into just how great he was! He is someone I have really looked up to over the years.
—*Terry Baucom*

Bobby Hicks has been part of the North Carolina bluegrass scene since 1948, when he first recorded with Jim Eanes and Hubert Davis. By the early 1950s, he had his first number-one hit and his career reached even greater heights. Bobby joined Bill Monroe and the Blue Grass Boys in 1954. By 1977, Bobby Hicks had achieved "legend" status with the Bobby Hicks Band, and the versatile musician showed no signs of slowing down. In 1981, he joined the Ricky Skaggs Band and was the featured fiddle player on the Ricky Skaggs number-one hit "Crying My Heart Out Over You." Bobby Hicks has inspired many fiddle players in the Carolinas and beyond. Ashely Carder (Palmetto Blue) spent time with Mr. Hicks in his home and said:

I had been a big fan of Bobby Hicks since the early 1980s when I heard his fine fiddling on the Bluegrass Album Band's albums and as the fiddler on Ricky Skaggs's version of Uncle Pen. I finally met Bobby in 2004, when I made a visit to his house in Marshall, North Carolina, so that I could learn how to play Uncle Pen properly. I had tried to get the fiddle part of Uncle Pen right for some time without much success, so I called Bobby's house, and his wife, Cathy, set up a time for me to come up. After driving up a winding gravel-and-dirt road through some pastures, I arrived at Bobby's house on top of the hill. We spent the afternoon working on fiddle tunes [and] talking about fiddling, about his years with Monroe, and he showed me the Georgia bow lick that was used in Uncle Pen. Later in the evening, Bobby asked me if I was interested in staying around a while and riding with him to a jam at Wayne Erbsen's home. Erbsen is a fiddler and multi-instrumentalist, [as well as the] author of several bluegrass books. We rode in Bobby's vintage green Cadillac to Wayne's home, where I enjoyed jamming with many local musicians, including fiddler Natalya Weinstein, who later married legendary North Carolina fiddler Jim Shumate's grandson John Cloyd Miller. It was a day to remember, and to this day, I

The Reno Brothers. *Courtesy of Bill's Music Shop & Pickin' Parlor.*

Lou Reid & Carolina. *Courtesy of Bill's Music Shop & Pickin' Parlor.*

*have to credit Bobby Hicks for showing me how to play Uncle Pen the way
it's supposed to be played, the way that Hicks learned it from fiddler Red
Taylor in the early 1950s.*

Bobby Hicks is a ten-time Grammy winner and a member of the North American and World Fiddlers' Hall of Fame. He is a 2014 recipient of the North Carolina Heritage Award.

MARC PRUETT

Marc Pruett continues to live where he was raised, in Haywood and Buncombe Counties, North Carolina. He has received numerous honors, including a Grammy for his contribution to Ricky Skaggs's smash success Bluegrass Rules. Marc also plays with the Asheville band Whitewater Bluegrass Company.

Marc is the banjo player and a founding member of Balsam Range, a sought-after group who released its first CD, *Marching Home*, in 2007. Marc was a recipient of the North Carolina Arts Council's prestigious North Carolina Heritage Award in 2015.

STEEP CANYON RANGERS

Since their days as students at the University of North Carolina–Chapel Hill in 1999, the Steep Canyon Rangers have drawn a crowd. Graham Sharp (banjo, harmony vocals), Woody Platt (guitar, lead vocals) and Charles R. Humphrey III (bass, harmony vocals) have found success honoring acoustic music. After graduating from college, Nicky Sanders (fiddler) joined the band, and they were so popular they couldn't keep their day jobs. It is hard to believe that a few years earlier, none of them was seriously thinking about being a full-time musician.

Original music has always been at the heart of what the Steep Canyon Rangers do. Sharp, Humphrey and Guggino have made major contributions, and the music has crossover appeal to everything from country and folk to rock and blues. Perhaps it is the variety that helps keep the group in such demand. By the time they graduated, the Steep Canyon Rangers were playing the club scenes and traditional bluegrass festivals.

In 2001, they released their first album, *Old Dreams and New Dreams*. In 2002, *Mr. Taylor's New Home* was released on the independent Bonfire label, and in 2004, the album *Steep Canyon Rangers* was their first release for Rebel. *One Dime at a Time* won the IBMA's Emerging Artist Award in 2006, and the title song was number one on the Bluegrass Unlimited chart.

The group is eclectic and did a ragtime cover of the Grateful Dead's "Don't Ease Me In," the album of which was also nominated for IBMA's Album of the Year. The honors continued. In 2008, the Steep Canyon Rangers played with Flatt and Scruggs vocalist Curly Seckler. Steve Martin asked the Steep Canyon Rangers to be his band on his tour to promote his banjo album, *The Crow: New Songs for the Five-String Banjo*. They went to San Francisco's Hardly Strictly Bluegrass Festival and have continued to work with Martin ever since. With recordings on Rounder Records in 2012 and 2013 and a 2015 release of their ninth album, *Radio*—produced by bluegrass legend Jerry Douglas—they introduced their sixth member, percussionist Mike Ashworth. Steep Canyon Rangers have always got something new to say as they travel from coast to coast.

FLATLAND EXPRESS

This five-member band delights its audiences with its captivating harmony and tantalizing instrumentation. The band enlivens its audiences with both traditional and nontraditional bluegrass and gospel, as well as stimulating re-compositions of older '60s and '70s music. All band members contribute to the vocal structure, and each adds his or her own unique mystique that provides a matchless sound for the group. The band includes Marty Carrigg (banjo, Dobro® and vocals), Otto (mandolin, banjo, guitar and vocals), Lewis Rogers (fiddle, mandolin, banjo and vocals) and Katie Miller (bass and vocals). The band was the 2013 winner of the Little Roy and Lizzy Band Competition and the 2015 third-place winner of the Renofest Band competition.

TOWN MOUNTAIN

Town Mountain calls Asheville, North Carolina, home and has been nominated for the IBMA's Emerging Artist Award. This group continues to headline at events like MerleFest. After nearly a decade of making music together, Robert Greer (guitar), Jesse Langlais (banjo), Nick DiSebastian (bass), Bobby Britt (fiddle) and Phil Barker (mandolin) describe themselves as a band that finds common ground between traditional bluegrass, outlaw country and pure old-time mountain music. They use the raw energy of modern punk string bands and are still committed to the high lonesome sound of Bill Monroe. You can't put them in a box, and they are recognized as one of the premier young American bluegrass bands.

THROUGH THE PAGES OF THIS BOOK I have shared historical facts, selected stories and treasured memories about the bluegrass community of the Carolinas. I quickly realized it would be impossible to capture the entire past, present and future within the pages of this book. A friend advised me, "You do the best you can, and let the rough end drag." With the help of the South Carolina Bluegrass and Traditional Music Association (SC BTMA), a page on the organizations website will be made available for folks to add additional information. We all know the list of Carolina bluegrass bands, musicians and festivals will take you from the "flatlands to the mountains" so please keep in touch!

To provide comments, corrections and updates please contact the author c/o SC-BTMA, Bill's Music Shop and Pickin' Parlor, 710 Meeting Street, West Columbia, SC 29169.

Bibliography

Adcock, Martha. Personal interviews. June–August 2015.

Ahrens, Pat. "Bill Wells: Bluegrass Music Preservationist." *Sandlapper Magazine*, Autumn 2002.

———. "Bluegrass Notes." *Hometown News*, June 2002.

———. "The Hired Hands and Bill's Music Shop." *South Carolina Then and Now*, South Carolina Department of Archives and History, 2001.

———. "Homer Lee 'Pappy' Sherrill: Master Fiddler." *Fiddler Magazine*, Spring 2001.

———. Personal interviews. February–August 2015.

Ahrens, Pat, and David Deese. "From Bluegrass Boys to Briarhoppers." *Bluegrass Unlimited*, December 2007.

Ahrens, Pat, and Jane Przybysz. "Music at Bill's Pickin' Parlor in the South Carolina Midlands." *American Musical Traditions*. Vol. 3, *British Isles Music*. New York: Schirmer, 2002.

Baily, Jay. "Historical Origin and Stylistic Developments of the Five String Banjo." *Journal of American Folklore* 85, no. 335: 58–65.

Baroody, Elizabeth. "Banjo: The Sound of America." *Early American Life* 7, no. 2 (April 1976).

Bellow, Roger. Personal interviews. June–July 2015.

Benson, Kristin Scott. Personal interviews. April–August 2015.

Benson, Wayne. Personal interview. April 2015.

Bibey, Alan. Personal interview. July 2015.

Blackwell, Curtis. Personal interview. July 2015.

BIBLIOGRAPHY

Cantwell, Robert. *Bluegrass Breakdown: The Making of the Old Southern Sound.* Urbana: University of Illinois Press, 1984.

Carlin, Bob. "High on the Hog: Fisher Hendley and the Aristocratic Pigs." *Old-Time Herald* 10, no. 6 (August–September 2006): 37.

Carder, Ashley. "Final Notes, Vernon Riddle." *Old-Time Herald.* http://www. oldtimeherald.org/here%2Bthere/final-notes/vernon-riddle.html.

————. Personal interviews. March–August 2015.

Chadbourne, Eugene. "Alan Bibey." All Music. http://www.allmusic.com/ artist/alan-bibey-mn0000629786/biography.

Combs, Josiah H., and D.K. Wilgus, eds. *Folk Songs of the United States.* Austin: University of Texas Press, 1967.

Conan, Neal. "Remembering Doc Watson with 'Tennessee Stud.'" NPR. http://www.npr.org/2012/05/30/154000832/remembering-doc-watson-with-tennessee-stud.

Davis, Shellie. Personal interview. July 2015.

DiPriest, Joe. "Last of the Biarhoppers Dies." CHS54.com. http://www. chs54.net/2010/09/last-of-original-briarhoppers-dies.html.

Dunaway, David King. *How Can I Keep from Singing: Pete Seeger.* New York: McGraw-Hill, 1981.

Epstein, Dena. "The Folk Banjo: A Documentary History." *Ethnomusicology* 19 (January 1975).

Ferris, William, and Charles Reagan Wilson, coeditors. *The Encyclopedia of Southern Culture.* Chapel Hill: University of North Carolina Press, 1989.

Ferris, William, and Mary L. Hart, eds. *Folk Music and Modern Sound.* Jackson: University of Mississippi Press, 1982.

Filene, Benjamin. *Romancing the Folk.* Chapel Hill: University of North Carolina Press, 2000.

Graddick, Jim. Personal interview. April 2015.

Gura, Philip F., and James F. Bollman. *America's Instrument: The Banjo in the 19ᵗʰ Century.* Chapel Hill: University of North Carolina Press, 1999.

Heaton, C.P. "The 5-String Banjo in North Carolina." *Southern Folklore Quarterly*, March 1971: 62–82.

Holt, George. "The Charlotte Country Music Story." 1985. https://archive. org/stream/charlottecountry00holt/charlottecountry00holt_djvu.txt.

Howell, Roger. Personal interviews. June–August 2015.

Hurley, Richard. Personal interviews. May–August 2015.

Klein, Larry. Personal interviews. March–August 2015.

Landsdown, Shirley. Personal interviews. May–August 2015.

Lawless, John. "Tut Taylor Passes." *Bluegrass Today*, April 9, 2015. http://bluegrasstoday.com/tut-taylor-passes.

Lehmann, Ted. Personal interviews. July–August 2015.

————. Ted Lehmann's Bluegrass, Books, and Brainstorms. http://tedlehmann.blogspot.com.

Lomax, Alan. *The Land Where the Blues Began*. New York: Pantheon, 1993.

Lott, Eric. *Love and Theft: Blackface Minstrelsy and the American Working Class*. New York: Oxford University Press, 1993.

Lucas, Harold, and Annette Lucas. Personal interviews. July 2015.

Lucas, Randy. Personal interviews. March–August 2015.

McKie, Tony. Personal interview. June–August 2015.

Nager, Larry. "Kristin Scott Benson with the Grascals: Cutting the Grass Ceiling." *Bluegrass Unlimited*, October 1, 2010. http://bluegrassmusic.com/content/2010/feature/kristin-scott-benson-with-the-grascals-cutting.

Niles, John Jacob. *The Ballad Book of John Jacob Niles*. Boston: Houghton Mifflin, 1961.

Otto, John S., and Augustus M. Burns. "Black and White Cultural Interaction in the Early Twentieth Century South: Race and Hillbilly Music." *Phylon* 35 (1974): 407–17.

Rogers, Jimmie N. *The Country Music Message: Revisited*. Fayetteville: University of Arkansas Press, 1989.

Rose, Carolina. Personal interviews. May–July 2015.

Sharpe, A.P. *A Complete Guide to Instruments of the Banjo Family*. London: Cliford Essex Music Co., 1966.

Smirnoff, Roger. "Gibson: The Early Years." *Pickin'*, June 1975.

Smith, Richard D. *Can't You Hear Me Callin': The Life of Bill Monroe*. New York: Little Brown and Company, 2000.

Thompson, Richard. "On This Day No. 8: Ballad of Jed Camplett." *Bluegrass Today*, January 19, 2013. http://bluegrasstoday.com/on-this-day-8-ballad-of-jed-clampett.

Tichi, Cecilia. *High Lonesome: The American Culture of Country Music*. Chapel Hill: University of North Carolina Press, 1994.

Titon, Jeff Todd, and Bob Carlin. *American Music Traditions*, Vol. 3, *British Isles Music*. New York: Schirmer, 2002.

Toll, Robert. *Blacking Up: The Minstrel Show in Nineteenth-Century America*. New York: Oxford University Press, 1974.

Trischka, Tony, and Pete Wernick. *Masters of the 5-String Banjo*. N.p.: Oak Publishing, 1988.

BIBLIOGRAPHY

Webb, Robert Lloyd. *Ring the Banjar! The Banjo in America from Folklore to Factory*. Boston: MIT Press, 1984.

Wells, Lousie. Personal interviews. February–June 2015.

Wells, Willie. Personal interviews. February–August 2015.

Wolfe, Charles K. *The Grand Ole Opry: The Early Years, 1925–1935*. London: Old Time Music, 1975.

Index

INDEX

INDEX

About the Author

G ail Wilson-Giarratano is the executive director and vice-president of the education-focused nonprofit City Year in Columbia, South Carolina. She began her nonprofit career with the Lancaster Arts Council in Lancaster, South Carolina, and the Museum of York County in Rock Hill, South Carolina. As a former performing and teaching artist, she has worked for the South Carolina Arts Commission, the Caribbean Cultural Center in New York and the Brooklyn Academy of Music in Brooklyn.

She holds a bachelor of arts in art from Winthrop University; a master's of science in leadership and policy from Wheelock College in Boston, Massachusetts; and a doctorate in leadership and decision sciences from Walden University. Her original one-woman show, *It's Cloudy in the West*, is based on family history and traces the life of a dance hall girl from a Carolina plantation to Dodge City, Kansas, in the 1800s. The play has been performed at colleges, schools, festivals and events throughout the

East and was featured at the Smithsonian Institute in honor of Women's History month. Gail currently resides in the Lake Carolina community of Columbia, South Carolina, with her blues musician husband, Anthony Charles (Giarratano), and their Great Dane, Adelina Bambina.